PASSING THE FLAME

The Life and Work of Dr Joan Martin

Joan

a wonderful friend

over many years

Joy Puritz

Joan

Aug 2011

Published by Green Oak Publishing

Passing the Flame
The Life and Work of Dr Joan Martin

ISBN 978-0-9555505-3-9

First published 2011 by Green Oak Publishing
www.greenoakpublishing.co.uk

Designed by Justin Spain

Copies of this book should be ordered by contacting
Joy Puritz, 149E Holland Road, London, W14 8AS
jepuritz@btinternet.com

The cover illustration was inspired by the oil lamp at
Hunmanby Hall and was drawn by a pupil, Sally Platts
of Form 3M (now Sally Strawson), for the Jubilee
edition of the school magazine of 1978.

Printed in Great Britain by MPG Books Group,
Bodmin and King's Lynn

Acknowledgments

Had this biography been on a grander scale, there are several other people I could have mentioned – people who have worked tirelessly for years, such as Eric Dilley who came from Holland Park School in his early teens to work as a volunteer at the Kensington Emperors Swimming Club and has never left. He is now its chairman, a long-serving club instructor and helped to write the book *Swimming for the Disabled*. He is also Office Manager of the Association for the Disabled in Kensington and Chelsea, and does the secretarial work of Halliwick AST.

There are many people who have encouraged me in the writing of this book, but I particularly wish to thank my friend Sandra Hempel Nibbs for her advice and for giving up her spare time to edit my manuscript. I must also thank Patrick Hastings and John Scott for providing much information, particularly about Joan's work with swimming. For checking for factual accuracy I am most grateful to the Right Reverend Michael Colclough, Canon Residentiary of St Paul's Cathedral, formerly Bishop of Kensington, the Reverend Rob Marshall and Joan's cousin Rowena Pratt.

Greatest thanks must go to Joan herself who not only allowed me the pleasure of delving into her fascinating life, but also the challenge of writing about it. Joan did a great deal of research among her papers and photos, preparing detailed notes ahead of my interviews with her. She would then make her throat quite sore talking for up to three hours at a time, giving me so much information that I had to ask surprisingly few questions. I hope this book will give pleasure to her and her friends. I have enjoyed every minute of writing it.

J.P.

Contents

1. Early Years

All through her early childhood almost the only thing Joan Martin drank was water. She hated milk or anything with milk in it, so her mother said: 'Well, there's plenty of water in the tap.' And that is how it was until she was thirteen years old when she and her mother were in the café at Rowntree's, the department store in Scarborough. Her mother suggested having a coffee, Joan tried it and was hooked for life. This life has been long, for Joan was born on 25 November 1915.

Her parents were Henry Martin and Violet Pratt. Henry Martin was a Methodist minister and Violet was a trained nurse who, when she married Henry, worked with him in her role as minister's wife. They met in Fulham, West London, at a prayer meeting that Henry was addressing and where Violet was singing a solo in her natural, untrained contralto voice. She had been born into a Baptist family but happily switched to Methodism. During World War I Joan's father was a padre in the army and therefore away from home most of the time, so her mother lived temporarily with her own parents in West Norwood, South London. It was here that Joan was born. Her father only heard of her birth two weeks later. For several years Joan only knew him as a photograph, and when he finally came home she never really bonded with him until she was much older and he was supporting her in her choice of career – unlike her mother who wanted her merely to be a good minister's daughter. Two years after Joan was born her sister Beryl arrived. It was quite an adjustment for Joan, no longer being her mother's only child. Another sister came on the scene much later, during World War II.

Beryl was by then a student teacher in Bournemouth to where schoolgirls from Southampton had been evacuated. Among them was fifteen-year-old Barbara Mountifield, whose parents seemed reluctant to have her home in the school holidays: she was the middle one of three children and seemed somehow unwanted. After some discussion with the school staff Beryl offered to take the girl to her mother in London – and the bombs. From then on Barbara was fostered by the Martins until she married, and, as it happened, Joan and Beryl seemed to grow closer to her than they had ever been to each other. Barbara kept in contact with her real parents, and at her Methodist wedding, conducted by Henry Martin, there were three sets of parents: the bride's biological parents, her foster parents and the groom's parents. Barbara trained in London as a nursery nurse and was a great support to Violet and Henry.

The Martin grandparents, James and Mary Jane, were living in Porthleven, Cornwall when Joan was born. James Martin was originally a tin miner but when the mine closed he and Mary Jane ran a village shop before retiring to Teignmouth in Devon. Joan remembers her grandmother as being quite a personality who kept her husband under her thumb. Family holidays were often spent with James and Mary Jane, and one of Joan's fondest memories was of being taken out on the boats with the fishermen. Once when she was about ten she was allowed to travel alone by train from Huddersfield to Devon to spend a fortnight there and then another fortnight with the Pratt grandparents in London. Her sister Beryl, who was less adventurous, always preferred to stay at home. She and Joan were like chalk and cheese: Joan loved outdoor activities and adventure while Beryl, although she later had a cottage in Wales and enjoyed walking, was more domesticated, doing tapestry and making cakes. Joan never enjoyed cooking and baking, but she did not mind cleaning and washing, and she loved dressmaking, which her mother taught her. She found this very useful when she was short of money. In her later years ('in my old age') she has also started tapestry, having learnt embroidery from Grandma Pratt as a child, as well as crochet and knitting from Grandma Martin.

Joan always felt rather spoilt by her Martin grandparents. She remembers her grandfather often taking her aside and giving her half a crown, warning her not to tell anyone, especially not Grandma. But then her grandmother would do precisely the same and also tell her not to breathe a word. She learnt at an early age how to keep secrets: if you gave your word you did not break it. She began to accumulate quite a lot of money that she did not need, and was constantly trying to find ways of spending it – one was going for a ride on the sea in a motorboat at five shillings a time.

Grandfather Pratt was Resident Warden at The Worshipful Society of Apothecaries of London before he retired to West Norwood. Until 1926 the Hall had a factory attached to it for the making of medicines for the army and navy, where he worked as an apothecary. The factory closed when the services started to get their drugs from Boots the chemists, but the Pratts continued to live there in an eleven-roomed flat at the top of the building. Joan's mother, Violet, was married from there: her wedding photos were taken in the Hall courtyard.

Grandfather Pratt was a great first-aider and was much involved with the St John Ambulance. He also had charge of the first fire brigade in any of the City companies. He had thought that the work with chemicals that was carried out in the factory could be a fire hazard and that the company therefore needed fire-fighting equipment. Arthur Pratt was the brigade's Chief Fire Officer and wore a splendid fireman's helmet on duty. The Hall is the oldest extant livery company hall in the City. Much of the building dates from 1672 when it was rebuilt after the Great Fire of 1666. The original wooden roof is one of the few original City livery company roofs to have survived the Blitz. A plaque next to the fireplace in one of the rooms tells how on the night of 11-12 October 1940, a 500-lb high-explosive bomb went through the roof and down a chimney to the basement but failed to explode.

After her grandparents and Aunt Dorothy, Violet's sister, died Joan took some material, including photos of Arthur's equipment, to the Apothecaries, who were interested enough to show them to the London Fire Brigade. The Fire Brigade had no idea that the company had had its own brigade. Some years later Arthur's fire helmet was discovered in an antique shop and returned to the Hall where it is on display.

About every three years Methodist ministers were moved to a new place, so some time after World War I the young Martin family moved to Portsmouth where Henry changed his uniform to become a naval chaplain. He did not go to sea but ministered from Portsmouth. Joan remembers with delight being allowed to accompany him on ferry boats on his many pastoral visits to places such as the Royal Hospital Haslar in Gosport (which closed as the last military hospital in the UK in 2007). The family lived in a large manse which Violet at once started to make her own, being talented at making cushions and curtains and planning colour schemes. She had an absolute horror of Victoriana and set about getting rid of the over-stated decoration. Joan remembers holding flamboyant bedsteads while her mother sawed them off, and large mirrors while she unceremoniously chopped away the superfluous smaller mirrors around the frame. Once Violet cleverly coloured stuccoed fruits with crayons, so that they matched her curtains. Joan was intrigued by her mother's ingenuity. There were sometimes terrible rows when Henry came home to discover what his wife had been up to. Joan found them fascinating rather than alarming.

After the years in Portsmouth, Henry Martin was moved to Lincoln. It was there that a six or seven-year-old Joan 'encountered' the Ancient Romans for the first time through the archaeological digs then taking place. She was so fascinated that she was sometimes late for her school, the junior section of Lincoln High School. She remembers one dig taking place under Boots the chemists; and another, of a Roman villa, right in the school grounds. Her father, who had been a teacher before he became a minister, always encouraged her to find out more about anything she showed an interest in. Despite being short of money he always managed to find a book for her on the relevant topic. He also taught her how to use a compass and a stopwatch long before most children learnt such things, and she was allowed to keep the compass, which turned out to be invaluable on misty moors. Henry would also point out landmarks and taught her to use them together with the sun in order to get her bearings. She is still always aware of her orientation in any place. Later, when she became a Girl Guide, she had to learn about the positions of the stars for orientation; and later still, in Africa, she found that the stars were 'all wrong' and that the sun set much more suddenly than in Europe, which she realised could be explained astronomically.

Her other encounter at this time was with the Anglican Church: not only was she attending a Church of England school but the long walk across town to reach it took her past the Anglican cathedral. Several of her school friends' parents worked in the cathedral, so the grounds became a kind of playground for her, and she and her friends particularly enjoyed exploring the subterranean parts of the building. She soon had a great longing for a cross to wear around her neck. Her Methodist parents were not very keen on the idea, and a crucifix would have been out of the question. She got around the problem by joining the Ministering Children's League at school, which encouraged children to do good turns for others, especially children less fortunate than themselves. The MCL badge was a little silver cross. Being a member of MCL sowed the seeds of Joan's later love of the Girl Guides, which was to become a hugely important part of her life.

The family's next move, in about 1924, was to Huddersfield. There Joan had to go to a council school in order to be able to take the entrance exams for Greenhead High School, which she later attended for about 18 months. At the council school Joan encountered real poverty for the first time. The conditions in this dirty, industrial town were a great culture shock. Many children in the streets and even some at school did not have shoes or adequate clothing. There were strikes, riots and general unrest, especially among the mill and mine workers, and this could make walking the streets quite dangerous. Sometimes there was a policeman watching the Martins' huge house to protect it from attacks; and although Joan was old enough to walk to school alone, she sometimes had to be accompanied, by the housemaid or an older girl from the school. Occasionally, if there was trouble on the streets when she was due to walk home, she would be told to wait for someone to take her, or to go somewhere to wait until it was safe. The weather was often very cold and damp, and in winter there was plenty of snow, which she had to walk through to and from school, even if it was up to her knees. Schools seldom closed because of snow in those days; most of the teachers and pupils lived within walking distance.

Her father sometimes took her with him when he visited mills or factories, so that she could see how things were made. He went there himself out of interest, and was allowed in because he was known by the management, something which would not so easily be allowed these days. She remembers the fascination of visiting a wool mill or seeing red-hot steel in a factory. Sometimes she went with him to visit sick or injured workers in their homes. Their poor living conditions were an eye-opener. From the maids who worked for the family over time, Joan learnt a great deal about the lives of those less fortunate than herself, such as the miners who did such a dangerous job down a deep hole in the earth. She was also quite put out by all the sandstone buildings, blackened by soot, instead of the red brick she was used to. She remembers walking the streets one day in search of any red-brick house, and almost getting lost. These unfamiliar surroundings and the shock of seeing so much poverty made this an anxious time in Joan's childhood. Her parents were constantly busy but they always gave up time for her if she wanted to speak to them about her troubles. To their horror, however, she began to pick up the local accent.

In Huddersfield it was a tradition to wear new clothes to church on Whit Sunday. There the children were each given a sixpenny piece as a treat. Violet was a talented dressmaker and made a lot of her daughters' clothes (including large taffeta bows with which she dressed Joan's fair curls), but she absolutely refused to allow them to take part in what she considered to be a kind of fashion parade: the girls could have new clothes at other times, but not on Whit Sunday; and they were certainly not allowed to take any sixpences. Small wonder then that Joan felt guilty and embarrassed by the half-crowns heaped on her by her Martin grandparents. A Methodist custom that Joan found rather horrible was taking photographs of the Minister with his family, which were then made into postcards and sold at the church bazaar. The pictures were either of a formal, posed group or a relaxed scene with the family engaged in some homely activity such as reading together. Joan did not mind having her photograph taken but she did object to being 'sold' to the congregation. Her father, on the other hand, rather liked showing off his brood. When he introduced his daughters after Barbara had joined them as a foster sister, he would get himself into a bit of a tangle saying: 'These two are my daughters, that is to say they are my official daughters.' Then he would hastily have to explain Barbara's presence without making it sound as if she were illegitimate.

Her fondest memories of her time in Huddersfield were of her bird-watching expeditions into the countryside with a junior-school friend and her father, G. Branwell Evans, who wrote country tales full of observations of nature, and was a fellow Methodist minister of Joan's father. What fascinated Joan was that he claimed to be part Gypsy. These idyllic walks were the beginning of Joan's tremendous interest in nature. She tends now to remember Huddersfield for the surrounding bluebell woods and the wild moors, each with their different species of birds. Joan discovered later in life that three of her cousins descended from her Pratt grandfather, the nature-lover and photographer, had inherited this affinity with the countryside. They had not grown up together but had developed their interests quite independently. One was Betty Pratt, who went to boarding school with her in their teens. Later in life Joan often found herself in the company of bird-watchers and always enjoyed opportunities to watch birds herself.

For about six summers running, during the Lincoln and Huddersfield years, Joan's father did an exchange with a preacher in the Channel Islands. The whole family would spend a glorious month on Jersey living in the preacher's house, and Henry Martin would have to preach on three Sundays. Joan found the journey very exciting: first hours on the train to Weymouth and then boarding the packet at midnight. She loved the old mail boat; nothing like today's characterless ferries with rows of airline-type seats. Beryl was instantly sick, but Joan never suffered (later, in her twenties, she sailed with a Girl Guide friend who had a yacht, along the west coast of Scotland, encountering many exciting storms). The house in Jersey was on St Aubin's Bay and Joan particularly remembers spending time taking rides with other children on the little railway around the south coast. At each end of the closed wooden carriages there was an open platform where the children would stand and wave. It was probably dangerous, but there were no bossy adults or health-and-safety regulations to spoil their fun.

Even as a child Joan had told her parents that she wanted to become a doctor. Several of her friends' parents were doctors, and in Huddersfield some of them took her with them on their rounds. She thinks that the death of three friends during her time in Huddersfield might have influenced her ambition to study medicine. But before this, when she was about six, she visited a little girl in hospital who had been badly burnt; she will never forget the smell of burnt flesh and has had a fear of fire ever since. The child mercifully recovered. But in Huddersfield two other sick friends she visited were not so lucky: one died of pneumonia and another of polio. The polio victim was one of the children who was taken to school with Joan by an older pupil. Tragically that older girl contracted encephalitis. Both Joan and the girl who later died of polio visited her from time to time. The poor girl ended up having to be wheeled around in a huge wicker chair. In the end she committed suicide. Joan told her father that she did not want any more friends: they just died. He said: 'Well, what are you going to do about it?' It was then that she began to think about her future career. All these deaths affected Joan deeply, and she felt a great urge to help in some way.

The family moved to Scarborough which was such a lovely place that they spent their summer holidays at home. Joan told her parents that she was sick of changing schools so they suggested that she should board. In 1928, the year the school first opened, she thus began her happiest school years – at Hunmanby Hall, a Methodist girls' boarding school in Hunmanby, North Yorkshire. It seemed like paradise. At first there were only about seventy girls, including her sister Beryl and her cousin Betty Pratt. Joan loved the relaxed atmosphere, the beautiful building and grounds, and being able to play lacrosse several times a week. Instead of the girls being divided into Houses they each belonged to a 'Manor'. There were four at that time, all named after former residents of the Hall: Cecil Manor (which was Joan's) and the Gant, Constable and Mitford Manors. The badges which the girls wore had on them the coats-of-arms of the named families. The school was self-governing to the extent that the girls were encouraged to take a share in the governance: each Manor had it's 'court leet' (a 'leet' originally having been a court in which lords of manors had jurisdiction over local disputes), which discussed problems and made suggestions or complaints to the higher 'court baron', the latter consisting of senior girls and staff. Thus the girls learnt early on the ways of committees.

Some of the girls' fathers were missionaries, but many were 'middle-management' – in industry and business. The school had its own Girl Guide and Brownie packs. This was when Joan joined the Guides. The school grounds were ideal for outdoor activities, where most of the guiding was done, but the girls would also join in local activities outside the grounds, including going away to camp. By the time Joan left in 1932 there were about 250 pupils, and the original manor house had been extended. (The school closed in 1991.) The assembly hall, which also served as a dining room and was extended to give more space, was the original main entrance hall of the stately home, complete with open fireplace.

The school symbol was the flame of an oil lamp, lit from the fire and then burning constantly on the mantelpiece over the fireplace. Joan thinks of it as symbolic of the Holy Ghost, which has always been a comfort to her; and she feels that there was another connection: the school was not far from the Flamborough cliffs where many ships had been wrecked in the distant past. Before the lighthouse was built, a beacon was lit to warn the sailors. The first issue of the school magazine at Christmas 1928 contains an account of how the symbol of the flame was chosen and the lamp ceremony came into being. Miss F.A. Hargreaves, the school's first headmistress, got together with others to find a suitable symbol or motto for the school. 'Miss Hargeaves, referring to a passage in the Levitical Law where the Jews were instructed to keep the light continuously in the Tabernacle, the flame of burnt offering upon the altar of sacrifice, suggested that that symbol of self devotion adopted by the Jews at the beginning of their life as a nation appealed in a special sense to us in our new life as a school,' runs the article. She pointed out that their school was not like a conventional one but more like a family, and that the flame could represent the family life that they wished to cherish. Another flame had been burning in their midst since the beginning of the school: that of enthusiasm, shown in the creation of the school; and, however united their purpose, disappointment and failure might still creep in. Then the flame could help them by symbolising the fire of purification, burning out all that was ignoble in their lives. Lastly, the flame could symbolise their devotion to God, as it did to the Jews.. God would light that flame in their hearts and they could keep it alight by helping to establish God's rule of love on earth.

Then the flame of their family life, the flame of enthusiasm, the flame of purification and of devotion could not only be kept alight within the school's walls, but could be taken out into the world so that each member of the school would be a 'flamebearer'. It was decided to keep the flame burning in the school and to repeat the ceremony at the end of each term to remind them all that the spirit that inspired them at school was to be taken out into their homes and into the world. So it then was, the focus of the ceremony always being the passing of the flame between everyone present, so that all could share in the symbolic act. The chaplain lit a taper from the lamp, passed the light to the headmistress who passed it on. As the light was handed to each group in turn: the teaching staff, the girls and the household staff, they repeated these words: 'May the spirit of this flame dwell in you, and kindle other hearts'. This always made a deep impression on Joan and she feels that it became the motto of her life. Since then she has always been thrilled when beacons have been lit across the country for special occasions: it always means a lot to her.

At the lamp service the school prayer was said and the school hymn sung, both of which were a great influence in her life:

The Flame Prayer

O thou who dwelleth in light unapproachable,
and yet whose home is the humble and contrite heart,
inspire us at this time with true devotion to Thee
and to the ideals of this school. May the flame of
purity, of unselfish love, and of wise adventure burn in
us brightly, where ever we may be, both now and in
the future years, through Jesus Christ our Lord. Amen.

The Flamebearer

God lit a Flame in Bethlehem
O Light! O Living Way!
And every Saint who held it high
Was faithful in his day.
And now the splendid torch is ours,
For English hands to hold,
That fires once lit in Galilee
May light an English wold.

Thus we would consecrate our hands
To the same shining task.
And call Thy Spirit down on us,
And for Thy Presence ask.
O may no unlit heart be here,
No feet that miss the Way;
O let no cherished hope be lost,
No bright love ember gray.

Lord! Fan thine ancient Faith in us,
The bearers of the Flame,
That every thought and deed may be
A hallowing of Thy Name;
That in the yet unravelled years
Flamebearers still to be,
Taking the torch from us shall say:
These, Lord, were true to Thee!

Joan and some of her fellow pupils protested about the phrase 'For English hands to hold': there were quite a number of foreign girls at the school, and singing about 'English' hands therefore simply would not do. This was a case for the courts leet and baron, and the word was changed to 'youthful'.

The words had been written by the school chaplain, the Revd Fred Pratt Green. It was the first hymn he ever wrote. He went on to be the most prolific hymn writer since Charles Wesley, writing most of his hymns after he retired. He had a great following in America, and people visited him from all over the world. While they were staying he would often write a hymn for them. He fell in love with the French mistress at Hunmanby Hall, Marjorie Dowsett, and they were married in 1931.

When Henry Martin was relocated from Scarborough to a manse overlooking Queen's Park in North London, Joan was sixteen and needing more rigorous schooling than Hunmanby Hall could provide if she was to study medicine. Her beloved Hunmanby was not able to provide teaching in many areas of science until more buildings were added in later years. Joan was heartbroken to leave but knew that she was doing the right thing in moving to the Maria Gray Training College in the autumn of 1932. This college was attached to the Brondesbury and Kilburn High School for Girls. Here was another new experience for Joan: the girls at the college, unlike those at Hunmanby Hall who achieved everything in a team spirit for their various Manors, were fiercely competitive and almost at each other's throats. There was no court leet or baron here, which made Joan feel that the college was quite backward compared to Hunmanby. Another adjustment was that having been a senior there she was now a 'nothing'. Showing her naivety in her reactions, in her first term Joan was often persecuted by the other girls. She tended to be better than most at sport, which did not bother the others too much, but getting leading roles in plays was to them life and death. Joan was so unhappy that for the first half of the spring term she lay ill at home with severe quinsy. Gradually she settled down, however, and by the end of the four years that she spent there before starting at medical school she was reasonably happy.

2. The Medic in Wartime

When Joan passed her School Certificate at the Maria Gray Training College she became one of about sixty applicants out of 150 to win a place at the Royal Free, the only London medical school that took women – and no men until the late 1940s. The medical school was in Hunter Street near Kings Cross, and the Royal Free Hospital, where Joan was to begin her clinical training just as war broke out in 1939, was at that time in Gray's Inn Road. Only eleven of the intake of sixty in 1936 finished their training in the minimum time of six years, as Joan did; quite a number of them had moved out of London when the bombing started and had to finish their training later. Joan did her training on a shoestring: she managed with the help of scholarships that she won, and grants that her parents managed to obtain. She also thinks that her grandparents might have contributed. She had sixpence for some cheese, an apple and a cup of coffee for her lunch in the hospital canteen, and one-and-sixpence for her evening meal in a little nearby restaurant.

Early in her Royal Free training Joan's parents moved to Ilford in Essex and she commuted into London. Later she rented two rooms on the second floor of a vet's house in St Mark's Road near Ladbroke Grove, North Kensington, with Joan Boyce, a medical student at King's College Hospital, whom she knew through the Guides. Joan Boyce had lived with her mother in South London, and Joan Martin had been allowed to live with them, but when Mrs Boyce moved, the two students went to St Mark's Road. Joan visited her parents at weekends when she was not on duty. One Sunday evening when she was on her way back to her flat, there was an air raid. At Liverpool Street Station she had changed from the mainline train onto the Metropolitan Line underground (now called the Hammersmith and City Line); as her train was coming into Farringdon, the station received a direct hit. All passengers had to get off the train and continue their journeys on foot. Everything around about seemed to be on fire. Joan would have gone into an air-raid shelter, but she had a scottie dog with her, and dogs were not allowed. (Joan had a particular fondness of scottie dogs and had several in succession.) A sailor, his kit bag over his shoulder, asked Joan if she knew the way to Paddington, which she did, so the two of them walked there together through the bombing, and then Joan continued to North Kensington alone. From then on Joan never felt safe on public transport during the bombing, and avoided it if she could. She had a particular fear of fire, perhaps because of her memory of the burnt child. Grandfather Pratt, now an ARP fire-fighter, was not too proud of Joan's fear. Sad to relate, some time later, when he was fire-fighting during a raid, he got so drenched and cold that he went down with pneumonia and died.

During the Blitz the Royal Free only used its ground-floor wards, and these really only for casualty and out-patients; other patients were moved to hospitals outside London. The students were on a casualty rota, ready to work at night if necessary. The shifts changed from day to night at midnight. If Joan was not on the night shift she would take one of the last Metropolitan Line trains to Ladbroke Grove. Everywhere was blacked out, even on the underground. She had to grope her way onto a train and try to find a seat, and was always terrified she would sit on someone's lap by mistake. One of her most vivid memories of St Mark's Road was of when the local gas works received a direct hit one night. There was a blinding flash and an explosion so massive that the wall of her flat seemed to sway inwards about a foot. Windows were, of course, often shattered, despite the tape that criss-crossed them, and they then had to be boarded up with pieces of cardboard until they could be replaced. The gas works incident was unnerving, so Joan moved to a basement flat in Linden Gardens, which she again shared with a fellow student. But she was not allowed to enjoy peace and quiet there either: as she was coming out of the underground station on the north side of Notting Hill Gate one evening all the buildings on the south side seemed to be collapsing. She had not heard the bomb but was in time to see its catastrophic effects.

At the hospital the students had a shelter under the quad where they slept when on night duty. There were just enough bunk beds for one night-duty team. The route from the hospital was through a basement door and into a rabbit warren of sunken passages open to the sky, which did not feel at all safe. One night when they were all scurrying to the shelter an incendiary bomb fell into this well, whereupon a student threw her sleeping bag over it to put it out, which left an awful mess of burning feathers. On another night, when Joan was in her bunk under the quad, all the students were called into the building to help evacuate patients and rescue as much equipment as they could. The students did not yet know it, but a parachute mine had hit the hospital and was dangling, as yet unexploded, from the roof near the operating theatre. In the dawning light of the morning it looked rather like a letter box. After hours of hard work everyone was suddenly ordered to leave the building immediately. Those in charge had known all along that the students had been in grave danger because the mine could have exploded at any time but their lives were deemed less important than saving equipment. Having spent most of the night working hard at that, Joan was blowed if she was not going to rescue her own most precious belongings: her microscope and her bicycle. She decided that the safest place for them was her parents' home in Ilford, so she took her bicycle, the microscope and as many of her other possessions as she could lay her hands on, and proceeded to cycle the seven or eight miles. She had had no food for hours (meals often went by the board during the bombing), but all she wanted to do was get away from danger. She had never gone by road to Ilford before, but she knew in which direction she had to go and just ploughed on. The worst thing about that cycle ride was that the whole of the City was cobbled; she felt so shaken up when she eventually arrived that she was hardly able to tell her parents what had happened. The microscope survived, however. Joan stayed that night with her parents and as luck would have it there was a bombing raid there that night. When there was a raid in Ilford Joan felt safest under the kitchen table. With her fear of fire she always made sure she knew the fastest escape route, wherever she was.

On the night of 29 December 1940 Joan and her fellow students heard that St Paul's Cathedral had been hit. When they came off duty the following morning they all mounted their bikes and pedalled off to see what damage had been done. To their surprise and relief there only seemed to be a little damage at the far east end of the building: the fire-watchers at the cathedral had done an amazing job that night. Joan now realises that she and her companions must have been a real nuisance that morning, pulling their bikes over the fire hoses and the rubble.

For a short time, when she was not too busy during this period, Joan joined the London Ambulance Service as an escort, partly to gain experience and also, as the students had to do so much unpaid work, it was a treat to be earning some money for a change. She did night shifts from a base near Euston Station, and had to keep to a rota. Occasionally this meant making an excuse to the hospital about why she could not do a shift there: she never let on that she was moonlighting. Terrifyingly, most of the work was in the docks at night during bombing raids, sometimes using laundry vans if there was a shortage of ambulances. The ambulance men, some of whom were not regulars either, were kind and helpful. Fortunately Joan had learnt first aid as a Girl Guide and always remained proficient, following in Grandfather Pratt's footsteps. After a few months, however, the moonlighting had to come to an end as it was simply becoming too much to cope with.

Despite her fear of raids, Joan was glad to be in London for her clinical training. The Royal Free students were on the front line in treating casualties and, Joan says, became budding surgeons almost overnight, while other students who had moved out of London to avoid the bombing had only the less acute cases to learn from. The only time Joan worked outside London in the war was during six weeks midwifery training at a temporary hospital in Buckinghamshire. Shardeloes House near Amersham was a stately home that had been taken over, and women were brought there towards the end of their pregnancy. Unfortunately a lot of them disliked the place so much that they returned to London to have their babies.

As a student at the Royal Free Joan got to know the doctor who was to have the greatest influence on her career, consultant paediatrician Ursula Shelley, a tall, dark, striking woman who looked as if she had walked straight out of Vogue magazine. Ursula was just the sort of woman who could make it in a career in those days, when professional women had to be either clever and glamorous or clever and smartly dressed, according to Joan, whose mother never wanted her daughter to be the 'suited' type. Joan says that Ursula literally 'brought me up in medicine'. She worked very hard for Ursula as a student and they became good friends, and, as it happened, went on working together for many years. Ursula got to know Joan's parents and particularly admired Violet Martin, who perhaps became a kind of substitute mother, as she did not get on well with her own. Ursula's mother had been one of the Royal Free's first women medical students, and, by a strange coincidence, Ursula's father had worked with Joan's grandfather as an apothecary at Apothecaries' Hall; in fact he had been in charge of making the drugs. Joan discovered this coincidence when she was visiting her Pratt grandparents in West Norwood and happened to mention Ursula's surname. Her grandmother then made the connection. It was through Ursula that the Apothecaries learnt of Joan's existence. (Women Apothecaries were not allowed until 1946 and still do not have the same rights and privileges as the men.) Joan was made an Apothecary in 1986 and is invited to attend their lectures and dinners. Shortly after this she was also made a Freeman of the City of London (which, contrary to a popular myth, does not mean that she is permitted to drive sheep over London Bridge).

One afternoon Ursula and Joan were working in a Royal Free outpatients clinic to which mothers were bringing their children. Although it was broad daylight, they suddenly heard a huge explosion as a bomb fell on the Church of Scotland near the medical school in Hunter Street. Joan was alone with a mother and child; she instinctively pushed them under the table and then saw the windows shatter. A conference was being held at the church at the time, and a number of people were killed. The Royal Free was inundated with wounded clergymen. Ursula called to Joan asking if she and her patients were all right. When Joan said yes, Ursula told her to continue with the outpatients clinic, so the mother and child were enticed out from under the table and Joan carried on. After about ten minutes a sister from the casualty department came up to ask the outpatients staff what they thought they were doing: there were people 'with their guts hanging out' in casualty, and all medical staff were needed. Off they went to do what they could for the almost hysterical clergymen. One was making such a noise that Ursula said to him: 'Pray to God, man, but for God's sake pray quietly.' One man seemed to have very little wrong with him; fortunately they kept him lying down because they soon discovered that he had a puncture wound in his thigh which could have caused him to bleed to death. The medical school had been affected by the blast and there were some minor casualties there, but no one was killed. One little old lady covered in dust had been sitting waiting for a long while. Eventually she could contain herself no longer, pulled Joan's white coat and said: 'Doctor, don't you remember me? I used to always give you an extra doughnut.' She worked in the medical school canteen where every day Joan had got her cheese and an apple; a doughnut had always been a big treat costing an extra sixpence. The dear old lady was almost unrecognisable under her layer of dust.

Joan worked until about eight o'clock that evening before all the bombing victims had been treated. Then the department had to be cleared up. When they were finished Ursula said: 'Oh dear, I was meant to be going out for a meal with someone this evening.' Joan said that she too had planned to meet a friend for a meal, so they went out for a meal together instead.

Joan's most traumatic experience of the war by far occurred when she was a junior casualty officer on night duty at the Queen Elizabeth Hospital for Children in Hackney Road, East London. Working with her on this occasion were a female senior casualty officer and two male medical students. Some time after 8.30 p.m. the department had a warning that about thirty 'faints' were coming in from an underground shelter. This seemed a very high number of people who had fainted all at the same time, and Joan thought that perhaps this was just going to be an exercise. As this was a children's hospital, the beds were small, but hospitals in the war had to have a minimum number of adult beds in case of a local incident. With the help of porters, the staff set about finding as many adult beds as they could, and soon the casualties began to arrive. To their horror all the first 'patients' were in fact corpses – mostly women and children whose faces were a pale lilac colour, typical of suffocation, and they kept coming and coming. They were often wet too because attempts had been made to revive them with water. The ambulance men said they had been asphyxiated in a crush of people trying to get into an air-raid shelter. A lot of the women's fingers were curled as if they had been grasping something as they died, perhaps a child or their bedding, which the women had to take to the shelter each night. There should have been a surgeon on duty for such an incident, and Joan never found out why one was not there that night. She thinks it might have been because the surgeon had been told that the casualties were all dead. Thirty corpses arrived before any living casualties turned up, and the latter were not serious, mostly with only a broken limb. These survivors tended to be school children or young men who had not been hampered by carrying children or bedding; in fact, one boy of about nine with a broken arm was able to describe to the medics what had happened and how he had scrambled out.

Nearby, Bethnal Green underground station was still unfinished but its huge subterranean spaces were already in regular use as a shelter, with at least 5,000 three-tiered bunk beds. Shortly after 8 p.m. on 3 March 1943 an air-raid warning sent people heading for the shelter, where about 500 were already settled for the night. As they were going down the poorly-lit stone steps, slippery with rain, a nearby anti-aircraft battery let off a salvo of about sixty rockets causing a huge roar. This was a new procedure and the sound was unfamiliar to the local residents. Although no aeroplanes had been heard, people thought they were under enemy attack. In panic many rushed for the steps, and a woman carrying a child stumbled and fell. A man tripped over her and, with everyone pushing desperately to get to safety, people began to fall on top of each other. (The woman who had stumbled apparently survived, but her child did not.) One hundred and seventy-three people died: 27 men, 84 women and 62 children, while 62 others were injured. Joan's version of this event, told to her by someone in authority, was that an elderly woman carrying bedding tripped and fell through one of two open doors at the bottom of the steps, blocking it with her body and her bedding. This left just one open door and people had started to stumble behind her in any case. Ironically, because she was half through the door and her head was in fresh air, she survived.

The ambulance men bringing in the corpses and the injured were quite frantic: many were locals and knew that their families might be among the dead and injured. As soon as they had delivered the casualties, they demanded the stretchers and blankets back so that they could go back to the rescue work. The beds that the staff had prepared filled up immediately and the corpses had to be laid unceremoniously on the floor. The senior casualty officer had a fit of hysterics, saying that her colleagues were disrespectful of the dead, dealing with the corpses in the way they were, and Joan suggested she was not in a fit state to work and should go home. That left Joan on her own with the two medical students. The three worked non-stop through the night, trying to comfort the distressed, treating broken limbs and finding space for ever more corpses by laying them on the floor of consulting rooms. They had considerable misgivings about this but it was all that they could do. Later in the night the ambulance men took the bodies away to the crypt of the local St John's Church, set up as a temporary mortuary. At eight o'clock in the morning, at the end of her shift, Joan was told that she could go off duty for the next 24 hours but that she should on no account breathe a word of what had happened to anyone, not even her family.

She was so distressed that she felt she had to unburden herself on someone. There was one person on whom she could: the consultant paediatrician at the hospital, Ursula Shelley, who by now was a good friend. Ursula lived with her housekeeper, Miss Gander, in Chiswick Mall, just west of Hammersmith. That dreadful morning all Joan could think of was that she needed to talk to Ursula. Not having eaten or drunk anything all night, she managed to get some breakfast in the hospital canteen and then thought about how to see her friend and where. Not in the hospital, that was for sure. As Ursula was not due home from work until late afternoon, and with Joan's fear of public transport, she decided to walk all the way from the East End across town to West London. She was wearing suitable shoes, the weather was dry and not too cold, and she felt that she needed to walk in order to work over in her mind all that had happened. She reached Ursula's house at about tea-time and had not eaten since breakfast. Miss Gander, a somewhat dour but kind person who already knew Joan, opened the door to her and saw at once her exhaustion and distress. Joan walked in thankfully, asking if Ursula was at home and saying that she was terribly thirsty and had had a frightful night of treating many casualties. Sworn to secrecy, she did not say any more. Miss Gander duly gave her glasses of water and then a welcome cup of coffee. Soon Ursula arrived from work in her car and listened while Joan, between bouts of tears, told her appalling story. When she had finished Ursula, who although kind was a strict disciplinarian, said: 'Right. Now we must never talk about this to anyone else.' They had a hot meal and Ursula insisted that Joan stay the night. The next morning Joan braved public transport and was back at work at 8 a.m. To this day she has a fear of being in a crush of people.

Joan is still in touch with Ruby Harper, Miss Gander's successor and who worked for Ursula for over forty years in the house full of lovely antiques that Ursula collected, and where she gave many lovely parties. Much to Joan's distress, Ursula suffered from dementia at the end of her life, but Joan always kept in touch with her and helped her whenever she could, unlike many others who had attended her parties. In one of her lucid moments Ursula asked Joan to keep visiting Ruby for the rest of the loyal housekeeper's life, which Joan promised to do. Ursula told her that she was leaving Ruby her country cottage and enough money to live on; she somehow could not tell Ruby this herself. Joan was a frequent guest at the cottage during Ursula's life, and continues to visit Ruby there, having spent Christmas with her almost every year since her own mother died.

For the last few years Joan has attended the annual memorial service, first held in 2003, at the nearby St John's Church for the 173 who died in the Bethnal Green shelter disaster. They are held on the first Sunday afternoon in March. Every time she attends, there is someone who relates to her; she might not know the person but they somehow know about her and the role she played. They often say such things as 'you must have known my mother'. One man, who was a boy at the time, told her that after he had managed to escape from the shelter unharmed, he was sent back down to join the people who had got into the shelter safely before the accident, but he was told on no account to tell anyone what had happened up above. A woman told Joan that both she and her sister survived, but that her sister never got over the shock and died in her twenties. Another woman said that every night when she lay down to go to sleep she could hear the screams of the shelter victims; being able to tell her story to reporters in recent years, and attending the memorial services, have helped her somewhat to come to terms with her dreadful experience.

There is a small commemorative plaque at the station, and a woman whose mother and sister were both killed in the shelter has worked hard to raise the thousands of pounds to have a sculpture, *Staircase to Heaven*, installed in the nearby Bethnal Green Gardens. This woman always lets Joan know about other commemorative events taking place. One was on the day before the memorial service of 2009: an excellent play reading about the disaster, which Joan found extremely realistic and moving.

So strong was Joan's instinct never to break her word and reveal a secret, and so shocked had she been by the event, that for over sixty years she never breathed a word to anyone else about what she had seen on that terrible night in March 1943. Recently she has been less reticent, especially since the media contacted her and she was interviewed on a BBC 3 television series, 'The week we went to war'. Her parents were never to know what their daughter endured. At the end of that frightful hospital shift she had phoned her mother to say that she had had a terrible night with lots of casualties but that she was unharmed; she said no more as she felt sure that her parents would hear about the tragedy soon enough on the radio. Later, when she realised that it had hardly been reported at all (and then only quite a bit later in one or two newspapers because of an enquiry) she knew that she could not say anything more about the incident. The authorities feared that this unnecessary civilian disaster could lower morale. Two years before the tragedy, alterations to the structure of the staircase had been recommended because of concerns about the possibility of just such an accident. These were rejected as 'a waste of money', however. Despite enquiries into the incident, no one was ever held directly responsible.

3. Marriage and Australia

During the war, while she was still a medical student, Joan met a naval officer through her father's connections. He was twelve years her senior and remarkably good-looking, especially when in uniform. She fell for him. They met when they could, but he was often off on convoys to the Arctic, so his visits to London were brief and infrequent. Life during the war was so unreal and uncertain: you never knew if you would be alive in a few days' time; nevertheless Joan was quite resistant to the idea of marriage. One evening, after the two of them had just enjoyed a dinner out in London's West End and were walking near Bond Street, they were caught out by an air raid. Suddenly there was a huge explosion and the officer flung Joan onto the ground and lay on top of her. Both were unhurt but this shock seemed to act as a kind of catalyst, for shortly after that Joan accepted his proposal of marriage.

They were married by her father in his Methodist church in Ilford. Joan did not change her surname except in her passport. Married life was very sporadic after that: Joan continued her studies and her husband turned up at her flat in St Mark's Road from time to time. It was a strange existence like many marriages at the time but for Joan and her husband the situation did not last for much more than a year. Joan's husband was in Singapore on 15 February 1942 when the then British territory surrendered to the Japanese. Joan cannot remember whether her husband managed to get away on his ship in time or whether he was taken prisoner and escaped. Whatever the truth, however, he ended up in Australia for the rest of the war and beyond, living very comfortably, and commanding that section of the navy. Shortly before the end of the war, when Joan had been a junior doctor for at least two years, he sent a message asking her to come and join him.

Armed with her medical certificates and a reference from Ursula Shelley, Joan embarked as a ship's doctor at Liverpool headed west for Australia via the Panama Canal, hoping to avoid encountering a U-boat on the way. The ship was a troop-carrier full of British soldiers who were cared for by about eleven other doctors. Joan's responsibility was for the sixty or so British women and children, the families of some of the troops. On board Joan made friends not only with the doctors with whom she took meals, but with some of the Australian naval officers and particularly their wives, friendships that have lasted years, and that stood her in good stead when she ran into difficulties in Australia.

Arriving in Melbourne was first of all a huge culture shock: having left blitzed and rationed England, she was now in a land not just of plenty but of reckless waste, where people hardly seemed to care what was happening back home. Her husband was very unsympathetic to her feelings and more or less told her to pull herself together: she was the wife of a Naval Commander now and was to be at his side for all social and official occasions, as necessary. Joan soon realised that she did not like the commanding officers nor being told what she should or should not do. After about seven months, she realised that naval life was not for her and she longed to work. With the help of her certificates and reference, she obtained a live-in job in a GP surgery in Sydney. This would be the only time in her life she would be a general practitioner. When she told her husband that she was leaving him and moving to Sydney, he said he would not allow it: he did not want a professional wife but a naval one. She left him anyway.

In the five months Joan worked at the practice the number of patients doubled: so many women wanted an English woman doctor. At the end of five months Joan wanted to return to England: there was nothing to keep her in Australia and she knew that her marriage was over. She did not tell her husband that she was leaving and was worried that he might get wind of it and try to stop her. With the help of the naval officers she had befriended on the troop ship out, she found a job, once again as ship's doctor, on the *Port Chalmers*, a New Zealand cargo ship on its way back to its home country and then bound for England, laden with New Zealand produce such as butter and lamb. Her friends smuggled her onto the boat, Joan expecting her husband to turn up on the quay at any moment, but she got away without mishap and knew, once they docked in Wellington, New Zealand, that she was safe. The ship was in Wellington for loading for three weeks, and Joan managed to explore the country a little and enjoy a holiday with friends who were living there. The ship docked at other ports too, and at one, on the west coast of the North Island, she had just 24 hours to do what she wanted. She was keen to visit the famous Waitomo glow-worm caves, and managed it in the time. She remembers being rowed silently into the caves at night and suddenly seeing bright lights all over the ceilings – the glow-worms. When the boat slid out into the open again the stars were bright in the moonless sky but not as bright as the glow-worms had been. Just the experience for a keen caver.

The ship eventually set sail for England from the north end of the North Island, heading east via Cape Horn; thus Joan never managed to travel around the world, since she had always gone by way of the Atlantic Ocean. But by going around the Horn they sailed in sight of icebergs, which was quite exciting. By now there were twelve rather grand passengers on board. Joan became good friends with the captain who was an old 'sea dog'. He told her that her sole responsibility was for him and the crew, not the passengers, so she had better not fraternise with them. She felt a little ostracised, and the passengers were a bit miffed too, but the captain, who knew what kind of people they were, had saved her from hours of boredom, for the passengers were tedium itself. He developed the symptoms of a stomach ulcer during the voyage, so Joan mostly looked after him. She had to put him on a restricted diet which resulted in him gaining a lot of weight. Luckily Joan was a good seamstress and altered all his clothes for him when it became necessary. Somewhere in the Atlantic they refuelled at a small island trading post. The passengers were allowed to go on land for some hours. The captain said to Joan that it was not worth visiting and that she might as well stay on board and relax, so as the gang of twelve passengers set off in a rather nasty little ferry, Joan declared she was staying behind. But then a message came from shore asking for the ship's doctor to come and see a sick child on the island, the daughter of the man in charge of the trading post. She was then rowed ashore in great style in the 'Admiral's barge', watched in surprise by the twelve from their uncomfortable ferry. The child only had a sore throat, probably tonsilitis; but the parents wanted Joan to write a sickness certificate recommending treatment so that they would all have an excuse to come home to England. It was impossible, of course. Perhaps they were sick of the place. The island was barren and rocky, with no trees or grass, and no source of fresh water. All water had to be imported. When Joan examined the little girl, who was not more than four years old, the child asked: 'Have you seen water?' – presumably meaning running water in the form of a stream or river.

When the ship had finally sailed from New Zealand Joan had received masses of flowers from her New Zealand friends. She did not know what to do with them, but the ship was equipped with many refrigerators for the cargo, and the captain had an amazing knowledge of which kinds of flowers needed to be kept cool at which temperatures to make them last. He also knew the order in which they would deteriorate, according to type and temperature. As it happened one of Joan's responsibilities was to check the fridge temperatures each day for the cargo and, with the exact temperature instructions from the captain, she was able to store the flowers so well that there were always flowers on the dining table for the six weeks of their passage, until a huge storm blew up in the Bay of Biscay. The flowers decked the tables in the main dining room where the passengers and, on a separate table, the ship's officers and Joan would sit. When off-duty, the crew had their own dining area. The storm was so fierce that both people and furniture seemed to end up 'upside down'. The captain was in the dining room instead of at his post on the bridge. The crew member steering the ship did not seem to know how to ride a storm with the result that they had been hit from the side by a huge wave. One member of the crew ended up with a broken limb and one fell down into the engine room getting quite badly burnt, so Joan suddenly had some work to do just before arriving back in England. They docked in Bristol where a case of VD among the crew involved a 'doctor from the court' coming on board. There was a lot of form-filling and talk, but Joan had had so much brandy the night before that she was in a daze and cannot remember how it resolved itself. The captain had been all for bribing the man to give them the go ahead to dock and disembark.

Joan's parents were very discreet about her husband; they had been worried about her going out to Australia and were delighted that she was back. They never blamed her or discussed the failed marriage with her; they realised that Joan did not know how long her husband was going to stay in Australia, and there had been no point in prolonging the agony. With the help of the cheapest solicitor she could find in London, Joan obtained a divorce three years later and her husband remarried. She could not be bothered to fight for a naval wife's allowance, which she might have been entitled to. Her ex-husband has since died.

As it happened, the husband of Joan's adopted sister Barbara and Ursula Shelley's brother had both been prisoners in the Japanese camps of Singapore. Barbara's husband had been a very fit young man, but his health was pretty much broken by the experience; Barbara being a trained nursery nurse was able to care for him, however, so he did not die until he was in his seventies. Ursula's brother was a doctor and therefore useful to the Japanese, so he was treated better than other POWs.

Joan revisited Australia twice in later years to see the friends she had made there.

4. The Doctor in Kensington

After qualifying in 1942, Joan spent six months at the Queen Elizabeth Hospital for Children in Hackney Road after which she had to rotate between different hospitals and departments every three months, as junior doctors do in order to gain experience in different fields of medicine. The Royal Marsden cancer hospital and the Royal Brompton in Chelsea were among those on the rota. Once she was able to settle, after two years as a junior doctor and after her year in Australia, she knew that she wanted a job which would leave her largely free in the evenings and at weekends. This was because she was very committed to working for the Girl Guides, of which more later.

Ursula Shelley, by then a specialist in cerebral palsy, was only too glad to have Joan working with her for half a day a week at the children's clinic at the Princess Louise Hospital in St Quintin's Avenue in North Kensington. Ursula believed that professionals should have interests outside their careers and gave Joan some advice about how to organise her working life around those interests, writing references for her so that she could find work at other children's clinics. Joan then went to work for the Royal Borough of Kensington under its Medical Officer of Health, Dr James Fenton. She was responsible for disabled children, keeping their details on registers, assessing them to find the most suitable school, and visiting schools and nurseries. The clinics were on weekdays from 9 to 5, and Joan only had to do one evening clinic a week and was on call one weekend a month. Being on call was in case of emergencies, such as on one occasion when a GP suspected that a man in Kensal Road had smallpox; Joan received a call from the Town Hall asking her to examine him. Mercifully the man did not have the disease, but if he had, Joan would have had to arrange for his removal to hospital, alert the authorities and go through other necessary procedures. One morning a week she would go to a school to conduct medical inspections. She preferred junior schools, and particularly disliked larger, seemingly more impersonal schools, such as Holland Park. She worked in several clinics each week on rotation, including a minor injuries centre set up in a disused pub in Portobello Road. The Cheyne Day Centre for children with cerebral palsy (some were weekly boarders) was also on Joan's patch. This then occupied the former home of the writer and political activist Vera Britten on the Embankment: Chelsea was by then already linked with Kensington as far as medical care was concerned.

The 1950s saw a big drive to immunise children against polio, and for a while Joan seemed to be doing nothing but giving injections. Having lost a childhood friend to the disease, however, she was only too glad to help, and thought how lucky people now were. At first some people were undecided about having the jab, but when a famous footballer contracted polio, there was suddenly far less reluctance to be immunised. A doctor, a nurse and a clerk had to go as a team to the clinics to deal with the hundreds who turned up. Joan remembers a clinic where people were organised in three queues to receive their injections. One man in the third queue suddenly asked: 'Do I have to have a third one?' He had thought he had to be in all three queues and had already had two jabs. Eventually lumps of sugar were used to dispense the vaccine. At schools it was important to be on the alert: sometimes a lump had obviously been spat out, and then it was a question of finding the child who had done it.

The 1950s was also a time of the 'boat people', or refugees, who arrived in Britain in their hundreds from places as far flung as Vietnam, if their boats had not sunk on the way.

Many spent some days in Kensington, staying in schools, until they had been assessed and moved on to other towns – or into hospital. Medical assessment was vital, so when a new batch arrived Joan was taken off other work for a while. Each boatload was under the charge of a professional, sometimes a doctor, who travelled with the refugees. These professionals tended not to stay in Britain, but went on to the USA where they felt they would have a better life. Some refugees were transferred to Peterborough, and Joan had to go there later to make sure that they had been adequately housed.

The Kensal Road area had been badly damaged in the war, so Irish labourers were brought over and housed there to rebuild and repair. Later they were replaced by Caribbeans, who are largely still there, along with many others including Poles, Portuguese, Moroccans and Cypriots. They were often housed in condemned buildings in an appalling state, with dreadful carpets and holes in the stairs. The families tended to have a TV but hardly any other furniture, eating and sleeping on the floor. Joan and her colleagues worked hard to get them rehoused. The organisation Campden Charities often gave money to alleviate desperate situations. Where the boat people were concerned, Joan had to work with adults as well as children, but the day-to-day work was only with children, and the immigrants had many. Joan can remember Moroccan families where the father had some menial work in a hotel; the children were at school all day and the mother was lonely and unhappy. The children would learn to speak English much better than their parents and would interpret for them; the mother, tied to the home, would have little chance to learn English. When the father had earned enough money he would go back alone to Morocco for a holiday, only to return with another woman. In the end a household might consist of a man, three women and ten children; and out of those children there was nearly always one who was disabled.

Joan found Kensington a good borough to work for, especially as the more well-to-do residents often gave money towards essential projects, and she worked there for the rest of her career. In her last working years she worked part-time and did locums in various places. She particularly enjoyed schools for the disabled, and as the Cheyne Day Centre was the only local one, she would venture forth to schools in Fulham, Hammersmith and Westminster.

Some time after qualifiying Joan rented a basement and ground-floor maisonette in Elgin Crescent, Notting Hill. Here she lived alone for the first time and was able to enjoy the Crescent residents' communal garden. She remained there until she bought a second-floor flat in Kensington Church Street in about 1980. It was at Elgin Crescent that Joan found herself looking after the 'royal goldfish'. Rowena Pratt, the daughter of one of Joan's cousins, had been governess to the younger sisters of the future King of Bhutan, Jigme Singye Wangchuck. She also tutored him and the older sisters when they were at home for the holidays (he was on the throne from 1972 until he abdicated in 2006 in favour of his eldest son). Rowena was subsequently employed by Princess Margaret as a chef's assistant at Kensington Palace. Joan would go in and out of the back of the palace when she was visiting Rowena, and one day she noticed two goldfish in a small bowl in the Princess's apartment. She and Rowena took pity on the creatures and Joan took them home to Elgin Crescent where she housed them in a much bigger and better tank. The royal goldfish had been kidnapped. Rowena later became a House Mother at Stowe School before she retired. Joan sometimes stayed with her there in her flat at the top of the House. When Rowena was working in Bhutan she was asked if she knew of someone who could teach English to the army officers' children. She recommended her younger sister Caroline who subsequently went out to take up the post, was married to a Bhutanese officer for a few years and had three daughters, one of whom still lives in Bhutan, as does Caroline. The other daughters live in England, where their Aunt Rowena keeps in close touch with them. Between Rowena and Caroline there is also a brother, Robin Pratt, who shares Joan's love of nature and is a keen photographer, like Joan's Grandfather Pratt. These are virtually the only relatives Joan now has left.

When Rowena and her sister Caroline were young teachers at the end of the 1950s, they became founder members of the Conservation Corps, an organisation of volunteers who work in their holidays at nature reserves throughout the country. Joan came to join them for a while one August when they were working at Minsmere in Suffolk, quite happy to sleep under canvas. At this time the Corps were successfully encouraging avocets to nest by building little islands in the water. Rowena's main task was to cook for the volunteers, and the meals were delicious. One perfect evening they had a barbecue on the beach to celebrate Caroline's 21st birthday and to watch for the first Russian sputnik, due to be visible that night. They had a wonderful view of it travelling from one horizon to the other. Joan also remembers long night watches for nocturnal birds at Minsmere. By coincidence, a manager of the Conservation Corps and therefore known to Rowena, was Brigadier Armstrong whom Joan later got to know quite separately and for a different reason: the Brigadier's wife was a VIP in the Guide movement. Joan came to know the couple well, and the Brigadier was able to tell Joan a lot about the Gurkhas. He had been in Burma during the war and had officiated at the ceremony of the Japanese surrender in Burma in 1945. A ferocious-looking sword was used in the ceremony, and the Brigadier was allowed to keep it. Joan used to feel uneasy when she saw it hanging in the couple's drawing room. Then their house was burgled and the sword disappeared, much to Joan's relief – and the Brigadier's grief.

Joan mainly knew the Armstrongs in their later years. They had hardly any relatives so Joan became 'their sort of junior faculty', she says, running around in circles after them. They were extremely good to her. After they retired to a house in Gloucestershire, where the sword was stolen, she often went to stay with them and did a lot of their gardening, planting for them every summer. The Brigadier was the gentlest of gentlemen, so when his friend Lord Mountbatten was killed by the IRA Joan was quite amazed at the violence of his anger.

By the time she was nearly seventy Joan had had enough of filling in tax forms, made particularly complicated by her many different work places, so she finally retired as a doctor. Dr Margaret Miles, who sometimes worked with Joan in North Kensington, remembers her as a doctor not ambitious to get to the top of her profession, but wonderful with children and dedicated to helping them, particularly those who were disabled. Margaret also remembers that Joan was very perceptive when dealing with foreign children and their families, and often took on the role of part social worker. It was not always easy to assess a child accurately if the parents were afraid of being sent back to their home country because of ill health. Also, in cultures where a woman is considered inferior, the father would be the one talking to the doctor about his child, although the mother knew far more about the child's symptoms. As Dr Miles says, 'Joan had her antennae out all the time'.

5. The Swimmer

Doctors are well known for being bad at first aid; many cannot even put on a bandage properly. Dr Joan Martin is one of the exceptions, having gained her qualification in first aid as a Girl Guide in her early teens. Her direct boss in Kensington, Deputy Medical Officer of Health, Dr Violet Russell, used to say that if anything happened to her she hoped that she would be around. One victim Joan saved was not especially grateful, however. As a young woman Joan was on a sailing holiday with a group of friends in the Western Isles of Scotland. On this particular day they were going to visit Iona from Oban. They were having a relaxing time, joking and laughing, when one of the women inhaled a sweet. When she started to turn blue Joan went round behind her, grabbed her around her middle and performed the thrusting Heimlich manoeuvre (or 'hug-me manoeuvre', as Joan calls it), making the sweet pop out of her mouth. The victim turned on her and said: 'Don't you ever do that to me again!' Her friends were all angry with her for being so ungrateful: Joan had undoubtedly saved her life.

Joan considered life-saving in water an essential skill. With her mother's help and without any flotation aids she had learnt to swim in the sea at an age before a child realises that it has to be learnt, and in her case it just came naturally. She was never a fast swimmer but a strong one, like her mother. Her father, who could not swim himself, was adamant that she should learn. Poor sister Beryl did not take to it at all, however. Joan learnt that if you get into difficulties in water or if you are life-saving, you must never lose your head, if you want to avoid a tragedy. On holiday in Teignmouth, not long after she gained her life-saving certificate, she helped another teenage girl who got out of her depth in the sea. Luckily the rescue was straightforward and Joan was able to bring the girl to the shore, but not without first shouting at her firmly what she should do and should not do. This was all-important and stood her in good stead when, in her eighties, she had to fish a bishop out of Greek waters one October. More of that later.

Again as a young woman, Joan saved a woman from drowning in a yachting disaster. It happened after Joan had left her husband in Australia and was spending three weeks in New Zealand waiting for the *Port Chalmers* to load before sailing for England. She was driving with friends near the coast, a man and wife with whom she was staying, when they suddenly saw the yacht capsize. At first her host carried on driving, but then he said that as it was a Sunday there would be no one about to help and that they ought to go back and see what they could do themselves. Getting anywhere near was a nightmare: the nearest point was a jetty that seemed to be for refuelling and had a locked gate which Joan had to climb over. Suddenly two men rushed up, apparently from nowhere, climbed over the gate, jumped into the sea and managed to pull a woman out of the water. She seemed to be unconscious, but Joan resuscitated her with artificial respiration (not mouth-to-mouth, which was not known in those days). The next priority was to get the woman to a nearby house somewhat uphill from the jetty where someone appeared to be looking out of a window. With great difficulty they lifted the half-drowned woman over the locked gate on the jetty and carried her to the house where Joan immediately took charge. One of the things she asked of the lady of the house was to run a hot bath for the victim. She noticed that the lady did everything immediately and without question. When the victim was able to speak she told Joan that there had been two others on the yacht. There was no hope for them now. Later Joan asked the lady of the house if she had been a Guide. She replied, yes, and that she still was: she was the local Guide Commissioner. She wanted to do something for Joan to show her gratitude for what she had done, so Joan suggested she send some food parcels to England, and gave her addresses where they would be most welcome. The Guide Commissioner was true to her word and about seven parcels were safely received. Joan could often tell whether people had been Guides or Scouts because of the way they dealt with situations. In disaster zones there are often Scout or Guide teams helping, in addition to all the other organisations.

Scouts and Guides as well as those working for a Duke of Edinburgh Award, and other senior school pupils, have proved useful helpers with Swimming for Disabled People, which Joan has been running for decades at the Kensington pool in Walmer Road. Until recently she was still going into the water with the swimmers, but had to give this up (except during the odd training session) because her skin has become sensitive to chlorine. However, she is still there as chief instructor every Friday evening, when the Borough allows the Kensington Emperors Club free swimming sessions, this being the evening in the week least popular with the general public. Joan formed the club in the summer of 1955 when she was treating disabled children in her clinics. (Their logo is an Emperor Penguin with a coronet on its head because of Kensington being a royal borough.) She had realised that swimming would be an excellent therapy for people with disabilities: because the body is lighter in water it is easier to move. Disabled people suddenly find that they can achieve something, and are sometimes further encouraged by seeing people with greater disabilities than themselves.

All swimming clubs for disabled people are grouped into regions known as ASTRAs. (ASTRA stands for Association of Swimming Therapy Regional Association.) Joan's club belongs to the London – North of the Thames region. Swimming galas are held in all the ASTRAs and, as the contestants have such a wide range of disabilities, they are carefully sorted, not by type of difficulty but by their average time of completing a race: the slower swimmers start first and the faster ones later, exactly according to their average time. This 'time system', as it is called, means that everyone has a chance to win. Blind contestants and those with learning difficulties might not be able to follow what is happening, of course, but this is nevertheless deemed the fairest way to organise the races.

The Association of Swimming Therapy (or AST, later named the Halliwick Association of Swimming Therapy or Halliwick AST) was founded in 1952 by James (Mac) McMillan M.B.E. Joan has been its Medical Officer for many years, and in 2004 was elected President. In this role she has often attended committees, such as the National Co-ordinating Committee for Swimming for People with Disabilities. This body was formed after Mac, with Joan to support him, went to the House of Commons to complain that not enough was being done for disabled people. The Government allowed them to see the Secretary of the Sports Council and look at a list of all the facilities in the country for people with disabilities. Sadly, there are fewer now than there were then because of boroughs having to cut back.

Mac devised the Halliwick Method (now called the Halliwick Concept) in 1949 when working with twelve disabled girls from Halliwick Church of England School for Crippled Girls, a boarding school in Enfield, North London. He was already a swimming coach and an Amateur Swimming Association (ASA) official, and had been instrumental in getting swimming shown on TV for the first time. He was also an engineer – he had mended aircraft during the war, which meant that he understood about the physics of buoyancy and propulsion and thus the way bodies behave in water. One day, before his association with the school, he was at a swimming gala attended by the Halliwick girls as onlookers and got to hear that one of them had expressed a wish to be able to swim. He took this seriously and in 1949 founded the first club for disabled swimmers, the Halliwick Penguins Swimming Club, specifically for those girls, and invited their relatives and friends to be trained as instructors and helpers. He called them penguins because, like penguins, disabled people move about awkwardly on land, but when in the water suddenly become much more mobile. By 1960 boys were also joining the club.

Joan first encountered Mac in 1954. She had often to attend lectures about help for people with disabilities, and that year she was sent to County Hall to hear two talks about swimming, one given by Mac. As a keen swimmer herself she was immediately converted and knew this was for her. Mac ran two clubs on alternate Sunday mornings at a huge pool in Ironmonger Row in the City of London and another pool in Finchley, North London. Joan worked with him at both, and admits guiltily that this meant that for some time she was unable to attend church on Sunday mornings. After the sessions Mac would take Joan back to his home where his wife Phyl, also a swimming instructor, would give them Sunday lunch, and Mac would teach Joan the details of his method. As Mac was not medically trained he found Joan's medical knowledge and advice very useful. He was absolutely convinced of the principles of his method and could be quite rude to any physiotherapists who questioned them (some of whom are still working with Joan now). The physios rather resented this as Mac was not medically qualified.

Joan tried hard to persuade Mac to make a film and write a book about his method because she could see how important it was to spread the word, but he was never keen. He did once publish a pamphlet called *Less than Fifty Shillings a Year* about his swimming clubs, this being all they cost him to run: he always insisted that the work should be voluntary. His helpers were almost all women: Mac found women easier to work with and any men who joined tended not to stay long. In any case women were needed to undress and dress the children.

Soon Joan was wanting to start her own club in Kensington, so she went to Medical Officer of Health, Dr James Fenton, to ask if she could use a pool in the borough to teach disabled children to swim. He thought it was a good idea but procrastinated. After several months of waiting Joan went to him again and said that if she could not have her pool by the summer the scheme would have to wait another whole year, as she could hardly start a swimming club in winter. Permission was then given almost overnight, and thus the Kensington Emperors Swimming Club was formed, named after Emperor Penguins so as not to be confused with the Halliwick Penguins. Mac used to come to their 90-minute Friday-evening Kensington sessions and then give a lecture to the helpers and trainers. Disabled adults are now part of the club, especially since the original children have grown up, and other adults join when they hear about the club, although they do not always stay. This means, of course, that men are now needed to help the male swimmers to change. Many swimmers are from ethnic minority groups and sometimes their religious holidays or fasts, such as Ramadan, prevent them from coming.

At first the swimmers were only those with physical disabilities, but soon children with learning difficulties began joining. Although Joan knew that she could not turn anyone away, she was somewhat alarmed by this, as she was not geared to coping with these children. But they often turned out to be excellent swimmers and, despite their difficulties, really understood what water did for them (even if they did not know why) and understood competitiveness. Recently a Down's Syndrome girl won medals in a swimming gala and Joan found her excitement a joy to witness. Nowadays, when crippling diseases such as polio are no longer common, disabled people are often those with learning difficulties.

Even when Joan had her own swimming club in Kensington she would still go and help at other clubs, such as Halliwick Penguins Swimming Club in Arnos Grove, North London where she met Patrick Hastings in 1965. Disabled by polio as a young teenager who had been a keen swimmer in Birmingham before his work relocated him in 1965 to North London, Patrick had found out about the club and met Joan on his first visit as they were both getting out of their cars. Patrick began as a swimmer but later became a volunteer instructor; to this task he added that of being the club's Treasurer before moving on in 1972 to become the National Treasurer for Halliwick AST until 1980.

When Joan had given up trying to persuade Mac to make a film about the Halliwick Concept she decided to take on the task herself through a friend, Bill Latto of the Town and Country production company. Unfortunately Mac tried to stop the plan by claiming that he owned the copyright and, as Treasurer, Patrick had to deal with legal wrangling. Mac spent a lot of money in the process but was unsuccessful. He was a strange mixture, Joan says: he so much wanted to help disabled people and yet, as is often the case with determined, highly-motivated characters, his ego sometimes got in the way. To help fund the film, many of the association's affiliated swimming clubs raised thousands of pounds swimming sponsored marathons, and Joan feels much indebted to Kensington resident, mover and shaker, John Scott for sourcing other funds. John's long association with the Emperors began when he responded to Kensington Council's call for volunteers to drive swimmers to the pool. He became very interested when he saw the swimming and subsequently trained as a instructor. For 25 years he helped swimmers at the club; now he still encourages young people to go to the pool and see if they might be interested in helping. He describes working at the club as having been the most enriching experience of his life, adding that 'Joan is so huge in the club as to block out the sun'.

The film, *Water Free*, was launched in 1975 in the private cinema of the Midland Bank headquarters in London in the presence of Alf Morris MP, then the first Minister for the Disabled. Patrick Hastings received a lovely letter of appreciation from Phyl Macmillan, Mac's wife. The film subsequently won several awards. Mac later had two short films demonstrating his method made abroad, and Town and Country distributed and hired them out in Britain.

Mac became increasingly frustrated that swimming teachers in Britain were not taking as much notice of his method as he would have liked, so in 1976 he left his wife and two teenaged daughters – effectively breaking up his marriage, and moved to Denmark and then Switzerland, where he died of a stroke in 1994. During his years abroad he visited England occasionally and continued to play a dominant role in the AST, sending tape-recordings of himself to be played at committee meetings so that members could hear his suggestions. Sometimes he would turn up at a meeting unannounced ('God walked in,' as Patrick describes it) and complain about what the committee was up to, saying that he ran Halliwick, nay, he *was* Halliwick.

Joan, together with other members of the Association, had a book published in 1981 which was collated and edited by John Scott, with illustrations by Haro Hodson, the well known British cartoonist and illustrator. *Swimming for the Disabled* by the Association of Swimming Therapy was launched in the House of Commons. John Scott had persuaded a charity to put up some of the money to help get the book out: the publisher agreed to publish if the then AST guaranteed to buy a quarter of the print run (which was paid for by the charity). When the books were sold, the charity was paid back. The book has since been reprinted several times and gone into three editions. The latest edition, *Halliwick Swimming for Disabled People*, was revised and updated by many members of the association's National Education Committee with help from others. It is now quite scientific, with detailed diagrams, and mentions the Ten Point Programme which is fundamental to Mac's ideas (in his lifetime he had insisted that only he had the right to publish the programme). Mac never forgave Joan for getting the book published but Joan feels that it is to his credit that he had not named the method after himself. Now his teachings are widely used, including by the ASA. Joan feels that credit is not always given to Mac for his ideas but believes that the important thing is that the method is being used to help people. Joan has been personally responsible for spreading the word overseas, so the method is now used internationally, and many swimming clubs around the world now belong to the International Halliwick Association (IHA). Most are Commonwealth countries but others, including Germany, Denmark, Switzerland, Slovenia and Japan, are also involved.

The Halliwick Concept never uses flotation aids: Joan and her assistants are the best life-saving apparatus the swimmers could ever have. Swimmers are shown that bodies never sink to the bottom but always float on, or just below, the surface of the water, and that the best position for floating is on the back. The old method of staying afloat by treading water is now frowned upon, as the turbulence created under a rising leg sucks the body down. It is now deemed best to keep the legs still and use the hands only for balance, either lying on the back or in a vertical position.) The swimmers learn to rotate in the water to get into the best position for whatever they want to do: float or swim. They are encouraged to put their heads under water and to breathe out into it. Some children become ecstatic at being able to see what is going on below the surface. Breathing and relaxing in water is taught long before actual propulsion through water or swimming. The swimmers must become 'creatures of water', feeling safe and at home there, sometimes with gentle physical support from instructors. This support must never involve holding the swimmer's head, however, but simply placing both hands gently under their shoulder blades. Even children with no limbs at all can still enjoy wriggling in the water, held by a net. Several children have learning difficulties, but they still enjoy the new sensation of floating. As with the ASTRA galas, the swimmers are grouped according to ability, irrespective of medical condition, which is regulated by a badge system. The instructors try to teach the children how to get in and out of the water independently, although some are never able to do so, of course. The introduction of hoists has made a huge difference: fifty years ago three people were needed to help a disabled person in and out of the pool (using a Transit seat made of canvas with three handles).

'Swimming for disabled people' was originally known as 'swimming for the handicapped', but this was changed when one of Joan's swimming charges, Menghi Mulchandani, a vocal Indian girl severely disabled by polio and very conscious of the problems facing people with disabilities, said that the word 'handicapped' should not be used since its literal meaning was 'cap-in-hand begging'. Joan never used it again but had difficulty during her travels abroad persuading every nation to adopt the term 'disabled'; the Japanese, for example, still use 'handicapped'.

Menghi Mulchandani's story is an interesting one. Because there was no provision in her home country for the education of disabled children, her family moved to England when she was five. She attended a school for disabled children in Fulham, West London. By chance Joan worked there as a doctor for a few weeks at the same time. A nurse at the school knew about the Emperors and felt that swimming would be the only thing that would help the child, who could barely sit upright, let alone walk. It took Joan more than one visit to Menghi's parents to persuade them to let their six-year-old daughter go to the pool ('we can't let our daughter be in a swimming costume among men!'), but she won them over in the end, and they soon realised how it was benefiting their highly intelligent child; in fact she was given a new lease of life. Menghi could only swim with a corkscrew action, which, alarmingly, made it look as if she were drowning: Joan had to warn the life-savers not to jump in after her. Menghi asked Joan if she could be her 'Indian daughter' and was accepted. The word 'daughter' in this context needs an explanation. When Joan went abroad to train swimming instructors she always needed someone to organise her itinerary, timetable and accommodation. She would ask the first person she met who seemed capable and available – perhaps one of her trainees – if she would take this on, and if the woman agreed Joan would jokingly refer to her as her 'daughter'. This happened a lot in Japan, which she visited frequently. She noticed that money was never a concern in Japan, at least then; the authorities just wanted to be told what was needed and it would be done or provided.

Menghi's parents ran a successful grocery shop and were quite well off. Just as Menghi was finishing school her mother died of cancer. Her father wanted her to stay at home and keep house, which she was perfectly capable of doing from her wheelchair but, wanting to be independent, she moved into her own flat and went to college in Hammersmith. Joan thinks she had the brain of a lawyer. Menghi then got a job advising disabled people about their needs, and went on to become Vice-Chairman of the Kensington Emperors and Chairman of both Halliwick AST and the IHA. In 2005 she organised a fabulous 50th-birthday party for the Emperors at Kensington Town Hall: a spectacular achievement.

Menghi's other achievements included being a founder member, and later Chief Executive, of Action Disability Kensington and Chelsea (ADKC), an organisation in North Kensington that is run and controlled by disabled people. She was interested in people with learning difficulties, and often seemed to be able to intuit what a swimming child wanted, and would demand it . She was often right. She could be quite bossy: Joan sometimes called her 'Mrs Gandhi'. In 1998 when Menghi retired as Chairman of Halliwick AST Joan telephoned Patrick Hastings, who had had to retire as Treasurer in 1978 when he moved to a house without a telephone connection for several months, and more or less said: 'You've got nothing much to do these days, you could be our chairman.' Patrick was unable to attend the next committee meeting, but Joan proposed him. He was duly elected and remains Chairman today.

Sadly, Menghi died of cancer in the autumn of 2007 when she was only 44. Her illness lasted ten months, during which time she never showed any self-pity. In the end she had to move in with her sister, where she celebrated her last birthday, organised by herself in just one week. It was a very merry occasion with lots of family and friends, and food and drink in the garden. No one had realised how ill she was until she suddenly announced to the company: 'I'm going to beat this' and whipped off her scarf to reveal a completely bald head. There were gasps of horror. Those months must have been difficult for her since she hated doctors – she would never admit that Joan was one. The well attended funeral a month later was on a Saturday morning at Golders Green Crematorium. As luck would have it Joan, feeling quite heartbroken, had to rush off straight after the ceremony to catch a train to Sevenoaks where she was to preside over that year's Annual National Swimming Championships.

Joan attends national meetings where people come together to give lectures on the disabled. In the autumn of 2010 she was one of the lecturers at such a meeting, together with Mandy Hudson, a very intelligent woman with cerebral palsy who was able to drive despite using a wheelchair. She had been on the Halliwick foundation course, which takes place over two weekends. Her talk was about disability awareness and how able-bodied people should deal with this. Afterwards Joan congratulated her, whereupon Mandy asked where Joan's swimming club was. As it happened, Mandy lived in Ealing, also in West London, and came to the Kensington pool to see how things were done. She was able to swim so she got into the water and Joan told her to swim around and watch what the instructors were doing. After the session, Mandy said she wanted to join as a helper. Joan was strongly reminded of Menghi. Having done the foundation course she is likely to do the advanced course, which Joan teaches, and undoubtedly become one of their lecturers eventually. Being somewhat disabled herself she will have to adapt some of the physical manoeuvres that helpers use with disabled swimmers, for example using the flat of only one hand instead of two to support someone under their shoulder blades, as she cannot flatten the other hand. Joan is very hopeful.

There has been another helper at the pool of some note. The Duchess of Cornwall's first husband, Andrew Parker Bowles, then still in the army, happened to be a friend of John Scott, who introduced him to the club. Andrew never went into the water but drove swimmers to and from the pool and helped as a volunteer at the poolside. His mother, by coincidence, was the Commonwealth Chief Commissioner of the Guides at the time, so Joan, as the Guides Training Adviser, would see her at meetings. Mrs Parker Bowles would occasionally ask Joan if her son was still helping on Friday evenings, and whom he brought with him. Occasionally he came with Camilla but never with Princess Anne, with whom he was also friendly at the time. Joan says he was a delightful person. Much later, at his mother's funeral, he made a point of speaking with Joan, asking her how the club was going. By coincidence, when Joan was awarded the M.B.E. at Buckingham Palace in November 1985, Andrew was the officer in charge, issuing instructions to everyone. The Queen put the medal on to Joan's jacket, where it stayed with the help of Velcro; outside, Andrew took it off and gave it to her in a box. He asked her whether she had any suggestions about how the ceremony might be improved; Joan replied that a cup of coffee at some stage during all the hanging around beforehand would have been welcome.

John Scott had got the ball rolling for Joan's M.B.E. award. Looking at her one day he had thought: 'Why hasn't Joan been awarded an honour?' He discovered that anyone can be nominated for an award as long as the application form is backed by character references from several people. John had no trouble finding people willing to write about Joan's virtues and good deeds, and duly sent all the paperwork off to the MP for Kensington, who proceeded to mislay it, thereby holding up the procedure for months.

When the Queen presented Joan with her medal she proved she had done her homework: she not only knew that Joan was a Guide (as she was herself), she also talked to her about the swimming. The Queen Mother also knew about the swimming. When she had opened the Queen Mother Sports Centre, in Westminster in 1981, Joan was there with a team of six Kensington children to demonstrate swimming for the disabled. They were supervised by a trainee nurse who was in the water with them. Joan was not allowed in the water as she had to speak to the Queen Mother who showed a great interest in all the children who were from various ethnic backgrounds. The Queen Mother said how relaxing she found talking to Joan in this informal setting; in fact she enjoyed it so much that she spent longer with Joan than had been allowed for. The nurse had to start the routine with the children all over again and Joan noticed that the Mayor seemed to be getting more and more agitated and was looking at his watch. Eventually Joan ventured to say: 'Ma'am, I'm sure you're meant to be somewhere else.' The Queen Mother replied: 'Yes, I expect I am, and I hope it's tea.' Westminster started its own swimming club for disabled children run by people trained at the Kensington club. For some time Joan would get a morning off a week to instruct there.

Prince Charles also knew about the swimming. This came about because Joan had been invited as the only woman to attend a ceremony at the YMCA pool in London where the Prince was presenting awards for life-saving. During the refreshments afterwards the Prince's equerry introduced Joan to Prince Charles, explaining that she worked with disabled people. He asked her if she was a life-saver too; when she said she was he asked: 'Did anyone ever tell you how to breathe?' She was very impressed by this extremely relevant question. She replied yes, and that this was one of the first things they taught the disabled, to breathe into the water. He said that no one had ever taught him about breathing, so that when he did underwater swimming for the first time in the Channel Islands it was quite a disaster: his breathing was not up to the task; the problem was, he said, that if you were royal you were not told how to do something you were expected to be able to do it.

In 1982 Princess Diana also showed a great interest in the swimming for disabled children and requested a demonstration at the Westminster pool. This was arranged in the junior pool, which was surrounded by a pit beyond which the Princess and Joan sat level with the pool. The children were swimming in such a way that they always had their faces turned away from the onlookers, so the Princess asked Joan if they could swim so that she could see their faces. With some difficulty Joan got the instructors to reverse the direction of the routine. The Princess then insisted on going down into the pit so that she could speak to the children. This caused enormous consternation as the pit was not particularly clean. Afterwards the Princess took the children on to her knee and was perfectly at home with them, whatever their disability. Joan was genuinely impressed. She learnt another touching story about the Princess from a friend who was a night sister in one of the children's hospitals: the Princess often visited, especially at night. During one of these visits, she had learnt about a mother who was constantly with her terminally ill child. She could not bear to leave her in case the child died when she was not there. The Princess asked her what she was doing about her washing. The woman said she could not do anything about it. The Princess took her washing away with her and brought it back clean the next day. Those were the sort of kindnesses the Princess was capable of.

Joan has lectured in Austria, Brazil, Greece, Ireland, Poland, Portugal, Scotland, Switzerland, Wales, and several times in Denmark, Japan and Slovenia; in a lot of these countries she has also trained instructors as indeed she did in Slovenia, in 1996, 1997 and 2004. Slovenia had become interested through Rajko Vute, Professor of Physical Education at the University of Ljubljana. He had a special interest in physical disabilities and had come to London to observe Joan's training. He had heard about her work through Nedda Rotar, a young Slovenian physiotherapist who had done a Halliwick training course in London and got to know Joan. When Joan went to instruct in Slovenia, Nedda was her 'daugther' there, although the Professor also looked after her a lot. In the course of time Joan qualified both of them as Halliwick lecturers, and the swimming training there has gone from strength to strength. She found visiting that country very interesting, especially as Nedda and others who were looking after her were very keen to tell her about the nation's recent history. Another fascination for Joan were the huge caves with stalagmites and stalactites. They were so internationally important that they were guarded by the army against terrorists, and they were so vast that one entered them by train. Being a caver, Joan loved to visit them, unlike the Professor who found them quite alarming: he would drive Joan the the entrance and then pick her up again when she came out at the other end.

Sometimes people Joan has trained abroad suddenly turn up without warning at one of her Friday night sessions to surprise her. Yo Kugaya, one of her Japanese 'daughters', sprung this on her once. For about twenty years Joan went to Japan every other year to train instructors. Her connections with that country began when a Japanese orthopaedic surgeon named Professor Yabe came to London and watched the work Joan was doing with her disabled swimmers. He asked her to come to Japan, but she insisted that a Japanese swimming instructor should first come to London to train with her. So Junko Egami, who was Japan's top swimming instructor and later became Joan's main 'daughter' in Japan, came over in 1982, 1983 and 1984 to work with Joan, for 2-3 weeks each time. In 1985 Joan went to train instructors in Japan for the first time. Both Junko and Yo are still involved with the Halliwick training.

Visiting Japan as often as she did, Joan became fascinated by the customs: even people in swimming costumes have to go through the ritual of bowing. Most important, you must be careful never to make a Japanese person look foolish. So Joan was having to suppress her amusement in some social situations. Junko would sometimes take her out for meals. When Joan was learning how to use chopsticks her hostess said diplomatically: 'We teach our children to do it like this'. Joan was intrigued about customs relating to footwear. The gardens in Japan are, of course, famous for their beauty. As in homes, one is not allowed to wear outdoor shoes in them but has to put on slippers provided, and if one sits on the tatami matting in a person's sitting room, one wears no shoes at all. For the sake of hygiene, other shoes are also provided for visiting the loo in someone's house.

Joan learnt that the Japanese do not like it if people will not at least try something new to them, such as food, for instance: it is all right to say you do not like it, but you must try. This was no problem for the adventurous Joan. When her hosts realised this they were encouraged to take her to the most interesting places. The Halliwick work was usually at the weekends so that she had time during the week to

Above – Arthur Pratt (wearing medals) with his fire brigade, ca 1900

Left – Joan's grandparents, Alice and Arthur Pratt in 1914

Above – Joan's grandparents, Mary Jane and James Martin in Devon

Right – Joan's parents, Henry and Violet Martin, on their wedding day

Joan in 1916

Joan in 1921

Postcard photo of the Martins, 1921

Postcard photo of the Martins, 1929

Above – Joan's parents in Scarborough

*Right – Postcard photo of Joan
and Beryl, 1929*

Official Guide photo taken of Joan in 1962 before she left for Africa. She is wearing the International Guide Badge.

Guide Channel Relay Swim, 1966.
Joan with 14-year-old Susan Oley who swam the final lap.

*Joan receiving the Beaver Award from Mrs Sheila Constantinide
at Porchester Baths in 1966.*

Joan with the Queen Mother at the opening of the
Queen Mother Sports Centre, Westminster, in 1981

Joan with her M.B.E. medal at Buckingham Palace, November 1985

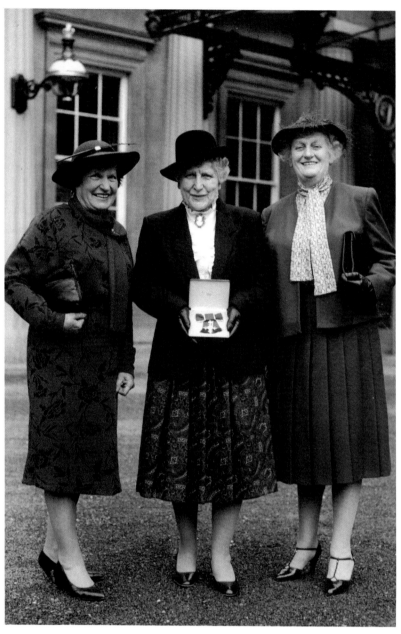

Joan with her sister Beryl (left) and foster sister Barbara Mountifield at the M.B.E. award ceremony.

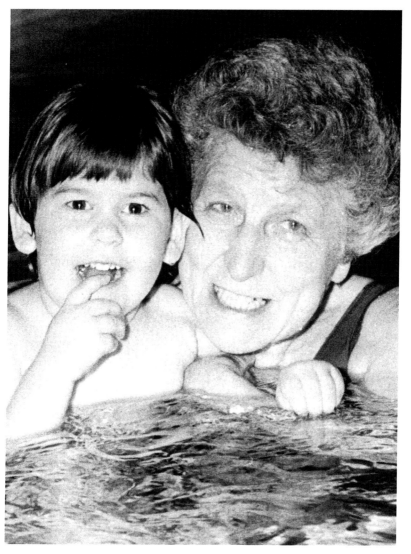

Joan helping a girl with learning difficulties to swim,
at the Queen Mother Sports Centre in 1985

Joan receiving the Mayor's Award on 25 May 2004 from Councillor Christopher Buckmaste
On left: Leader of the Council, Councillor Merrick Cockell.

With the Girl Scouts at Levos, 2006. Joan (seated centre); Bishop Michael and Cynthia
Colclough (back row); Ailsie Corbell (second row, far right).

Joan receiving the St Mellitus Medal from Bishop Michael on 24 May 2007.

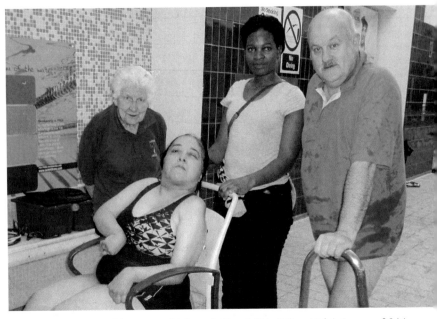

A swimmer and her carer, with Joan (left) and Eric Dilley (right), January 2011

Joan instructing Mandy Hudson, January 2011

see something of the country, and her hosts proudly took her absolutely anywhere – including to brothels, which are legal there. There is, however, much more to them than prostitution: they have lots of entertainment on offer. One in Kyoto, whose Madame was the mother of one of Joan's students, was surrounded by a high wall. Going through the door was like going into a prison but then the first thing you saw was a beautiful garden where food was served; then a room for practising music, then relaxation rooms; finally you would see the rooms where the customers were served in the way intended.

On one visit to Japan, in 2004, Joan was accompanied by Pamela Wood, a Major in the Salvation Army. Joan had encouraged her to be a volunteer at the swimming club, which she did for many years. As Pamela was used to public speaking in the Salvation Army she eventually became a senior lecturer on the Halliwick Concept. In Japan, she helped Joan with the testing of the would-be swimming trainers. She now lives in Devon, and they have remained very good friends, visiting each other regularly. Pamela also came on some of the Christian pilgrimages which Joan has undertaken.

Joan does not understand any Japanese, which proved her downfall, literally, when in 1992 she was getting off one of Japan's high-speed trains, which were technically way ahead of anything in England at the time. It was when she had undertaken a day trip to a university where she had had to give a lecture, after which she had been showered with gifts. She was then rather encumbered with these on her return journey to Kyoto, which she made with one of her Japanese 'daughters' who always had to accompany her. Normally the trains were so aligned to the platforms that there was no gap or step when boarding or alighting, but it so happened that this time there was a gap just where she had to get off;

she was carrying the parcels and a lot of other people were also getting off. Unable to understand any warning signs or announcements to mind the gap, she ended up with her left leg right down between the platform and the train. An official on the platform in front of her looked horrified and immediately pulled her out. A lot of the skin on her shin had been scraped right off, and Joan had to have it dressed by a doctor. He gave her something to put on the wounds, but it was so painful that she soon resorted to salt water. She had no choice but to carry on with her work for the next two or three weeks although she was now unable to do any more swimming, simply supervising from the poolside.

She booked an extra seat on her flight home so that she could keep her leg up on it; but not long into the flight the cabin crew, knowing from the passenger list that she was a doctor, asked her to attend to another passenger who had collapsed with a heart attack. The attack was not acute but Joan had to sit with the man for hours, keep him upright and calm, and stop the stewardesses from giving him brandy, which they seemed determined to do. From having been a patient herself she was now a doctor again and had to forget about her painful leg. On landing in England an ambulance was waiting for the heart patient. Joan was given a bottle of champagne on leaving the plane and later received a letter of thanks from Virgin Atlantic. In England a few weeks later when the leg had still failed to heal, despite the ministrations of a district nurse, Joan was admitted to Charing Cross Hospital for two or three weeks. She took with her the proofs of the second edition of the swimming book, much to the amusement of the staff. Annoyingly, she was unable to take up an invitation to watch the tennis at Wimbledon at that time. In the end she had to have skin grafts, with skin from her left thigh being grafted onto the left shin. Patrick Hastings and his wife Marjorie fetched her from hospital and took her to convalesce in their home near St Alban's. They already had Marjorie's father staying, so Joan had to sleep on a mattress on Patrick's office floor.

The summer weather was beautiful and they had a lot of their meals outside. Joan loved working in the garden (which she regularly did when she visited) but so did Marjorie's father, and there was an amusing contest between the two, who were always trying to beat each other into the garden first thing in the morning. Joan has no problem getting up early, so she would always try to get into the garden before him, then he would do the same, and the starting time would get earlier and earlier until it reached about 5.30. Joan says that Marjorie's father tended to weed the wrong plants but she also admits that it was a case of one-upmanship.

Joan also remembers the fun she had in 1968, when the Hastings had just moved to Potters Bar. On Sunday mornings Joan, with Mac and Phyl McMillan, ran training sessions in the local Barracuda Swimming Club which Marjorie and Patrick Hastings had recently helped to found. At the time an archaeological dig was taking place at the Roman site of Verulamium, near St Alban's. Joan had been interested in the digs in Lincoln when she lived there as a child, and always had a fascination for the Romans. Now she found she could participate: she and the McMillans would bring finds such as pottery shards back to the Hastings' house and scrub them clean before returning them to the site. But for Joan the most exciting and dramatic find at Verulamium was the amphitheatre. There had not been one in Lincoln, and there are few to be found in Britain generally, but here at last she saw her first.

Since Marjorie died in March 2010 Joan always phones Patrick on a Friday morning to see how he is getting on. She and Patrick also have mutual friends in Norfolk, and, visiting his second home there at least once a month, he sometimes drives her there to stay for the weekend. One of the mutual friends they would visit, until he died in 2000, was the Revd Fred Pratt Green, Joan's school chaplain at Hunmanby Hall with whom she had stayed in touch since she had left the school. She only found out later that his courtship of the French mistress had mostly taken place in Joan's parents' house in Scarborough, only a few miles away. As the two of them were both living at the school, they had nowhere to be private, and as a Methodist the chaplain knew Joan's father. He would go to Henry and Violet for tea and bring Marjorie Dowsett along. At the end of his life Pratt Green lived in a nursing home in Norwich. Joan and the Hastings would take him out to a pub, which he loved.

When the Hastings first started going to Norfolk they stayed in hotels, but in 1993 they fell in love with a semi-detached 250-year-old cottage in Pulham Market, just south of Norwich, Patrick's birthplace. One Sunday they drove Joan down to inspect it before the purchase, which they then decided on that very day. The local people have always been wonderfully friendly and helpful, and Joan was able to introduce the Hastings to Anna Meek, a Queen's Guide whom Joan had known since 1952 when, as Anna Dilley, she had been a lieutenant in Joan's local Guide group, The 1st Paddington, and who had also helped with the swimming club. She had ended up living just eleven miles away in Wymondham. Joan explained that 'Queen's Guide' is a Guiding award, not unlike the Duke of Edinburgh's Award, which is achieved after the Second and First Class Badges.

The Mayor of Kensington and Chelsea is always the President of the Kensington Emperors, so he, of course, was present at the grand 50th-birthday celebrations. Joan is often invited to Borough functions. She says the Borough is always very fair and quite proud of what the club is doing; it is quite an expense for the Council, of course, but this has never interfered with the way the club is run. Originally it said it could only provide transport three weeks out of four, which would have made life difficult, since private transport was quite inadequate; but somehow the transport simply turned up every week after all. If Joan needs anything from the Borough she contacts Councillor Christopher Buckmaster, who always does what he says he will do and whom she holds in high regard.

On 20th May 2004 Joan received the Mayor's Award from the Borough 'for services to swimming for the disabled, particularly in setting up the Kensington Emperors Swimming Club'.

6. The Guider

Joan was enrolled as a Girl Guide in 1929 at her beloved Hunmanby Hall School at the age of thirteen. It so happened that the headmistress was determined to have Girl Guides, Brownies and Rangers at the school, and selected staff who had had appropriate training. Joan learnt the Guiding promise: to love God, serve King and country, help others and keep the Guide Law. Even if it rained a lot she loved camping, which took place at the end of each summer term. Later, aged sixteen, when she was at college in London and miserable at having had to leave her boarding school, Guiding was her main consolation. She became a lieutenant and helped to run The 1st Paddington, the Guide company attached to her father's church, Fernhead Road Methodist Church. Later, when she was a medical student, she became Captain of that company, and finally, in her late twenties, Guide Commissioner for Paddington. This led to her becoming a training adviser at around the same time as she qualified as a doctor

As a sixteen-year-old she thoroughly enjoyed taking the under-privileged girls to camp, which was run by other Paddington Guiders (a Guider being a Guides officer). Some of the children were experiencing the countryside for the first time in their lives. To be qualified to take the girls she had to pass exams in first aid, life-saving, resuscitation, home nursing, tent-pitching and cooking. She found most of these qualifications invaluable in later life, realising that she would not have learnt them otherwise, except perhaps for cooking, which she did not enjoy: the night before the cooking exam she could hardly sleep as she was worried she might be asked to make porridge, or something equally problematic (she loathes porridge).

Within a few years she gained her camper's licence, which allowed her to be in charge of camping expeditions. Joan never really had much to do with Brownies or Rangers, the latter aged about 16-25; she was always happiest with the Girl Guides, aged early to mid-teens, as she felt she understood this age group best. She took girls camping all through the war: as they camped in the countryside, usually in Buckinghamshire, it was considered safe enough. On Easter and Whitsun weekends she would camp with senior Guides to prepare them for their responsibilities in the summer when they took the young Guides camping. Joan loved to sleep outside the tent if possible, so that she could look at the stars. Quite often, if she spotted a very special star, she would wake up any of her friends who were also sleeping outside and tell them to have a look. They were not best pleased. At that time they used ex-army bell (bell-shaped) tents that they could buy for about £5 (the Guide companies bought their own equipment); later they used ridge tents. At that time their company's equipment was stored in the stables of Hall Barn, Beaconsfield, the home of Lady Burnham, Chief Guide Commissioner for England. Later the company built a hut for the purpose. Lord Burnham, riding round his estate, would sometimes visit the camp out of curiosity. Joan remembers a small Guide rushing up to her and exclaiming: 'There's the Lord on an 'orse!' Joan was glad that for at least one week in the year the girls would have the chance to eat what she considered to be 'proper' food. Interestingly, they disliked butter, saying that it was tasteless compared with the margarine they were used to; similarly fresh milk seemed tasteless compared with their usual sterilised milk. When the Guides held their meetings in camp they always sat in a horseshoe formation so that everyone could be heard. Once when they were camping in Ibstone, Joan said that the horseshoe should be formed in such a way that all the Guides could see the lovely view. One small Guide asked her: 'What's a view?' The poor child had no concept of it.

Although Joan was happiest with Guides, she also had the opportunity to work with the Rangers. Originally these were split into groups: Rangers, Air Rangers and Sea Rangers, but after a while they were amalgamated simply as Rangers. It was with the Rangers that Joan was able to enjoy climbing and caving, as the adult in charge. This involved weekends in the Peak and Lake Districts where she and the girls were taught by experts, usually men. She found it fascinating how the girls, many away from home for the first time, found the courage to take on these quite challenging activities. Joan never led the climbing and caving expeditions, this was the task of an expert, but she would bring up the rear. On one occasion when they were underground and had had quite a difficult time, one girl was suddenly afraid to go on, so Joan told her that she would stay with her until the girl felt able to continue. In the end she managed it. Joan found this group psychology absolutely fascinating.

Joan's parents always encouraged her in these activities – within reason: caving was all right, but they drew the line at potholing. Caving involves walking straight into a cave from ground level, but potholing means descending into the cave for some distance by rope or ladder. When Joan became Guide Training Adviser for England, which involved lecturing and demonstration, at a time when the Guides had much to do in catching up with the activities of the Scouts, Joan introduced some commando-type activities, such as making and using rope-ladders and rope-bridges. She worked with the Scouts to learn how this was done. The reward was great: crossing a river on a rope bridge was utterly thrilling, she found. It was also a huge responsibility since she would have been blamed for any accidents. She always made sure that there was insurance cover.

Another aspect of Guiding that fascinated her was the international one: Guides from other countries often came on visits. Joan remembers the Girl Guides World Camp of 1957, held in Windsor Great Park to mark the centenary of Lord Baden-Powell's birth. Four thousand Guides took part. Joan was appointed camp doctor under another medical officer. She loves pomp and ceremony, flags and badges, and whenever the camp 'hospital' seemed quiet she would slip out to attend any ceremonies taking place. Her senior colleague probably got rather browned off with this and gradually absented herself more and more until Joan was left virtually in charge. There was always plenty to do, in bursts. She remembers being dismayed by the Danish Guides' bands playing from nine at night, keeping the other guides awake. At their age, they all needed plenty of sleep. But there was nothing she could do: the Danes were 'irrepressible'. The Chief Guide and Mary, Princess Royal were official visitors, and Joan's first introduction to the Queen was here when Her Majesty and the Duke of Edinburgh visited both the camp and its hospital. The senior medical officer might well have kicked herself when that happened.

Joan also did a lot of Guiding for girls from other countries at the international chalet at Adelboden, in the Bernese Oberland of Switzerland. After the war a great Guiding friend, Penelope or 'Pen', who worked at Guide HQ and was in charge of the chalet, persuaded Joan to join her there to help on skiing trips in the winter and walking trips in the summer. Joan, by now in her forties, thought she was a little old to learn to ski, but she managed well enough, and once she had learned what was involved in taking groups skiing and walking, she was able, year on year, to take parties of Guides to the chalet. As with the caving, she did not lead the parties but went as first-aider and brought up the rear. When going out with the skiing parties she more often than not ended up giving first aid to other people they encountered rather than to her own Guides. She felt a bit like a St Bernard, rushing to help. If she spotted a huddle of people she always knew something was wrong, and, being a Guide, it was her duty to help. It was mostly a case of dislocated shoulders or twisted ankles. Shoulders could be put back in place on the spot and, with the help of a first-aid kit, ankles could be strapped up. The chalet people always had a good relationship with the locals so, if necessary, a message could be sent to them asking for a sledge to come and take a casualty away.

The most serious incident Joan experienced involved herself and the ski leader, Inge, an experienced Danish woman. After they had finished taking a party skiing and sent them back to the chalet, they decided to go off-piste together for the rest of the afternoon. The sun was shining and they were keen to get some skiing in without being hampered by beginners, but they failed to notice how the air temperature was rising. After a while they saw that the snow they had just been skiing on was sliding downhill. They were setting off avalanches. They skied on, trying to get to a better level, when suddenly the whole slope in front of them was dislodged before their eyes. Soon they were disappearing with it, but because they were at the top of the avalanche, they always stayed above the worst of it; by keeping upright and side-slipping they did not break or lose their skis and kept shouting to each other through the snow clouds and above the roar of the avalanche to check where the other was. Eventually they came to a halt in a gully. As a good Guide Joan did not try to have any bright ideas herself but followed Inge's instructions exactly, so that eventually they sorted themselves out and got out of the gully and skied down to try and catch the last bus back.

There at the bus stop stood the rotund local pastor (who eventually married Pen, as it happened). They had told him at lunchtime what they were going to do that afternoon, and he knew that they were not yet off the mountain, and so had stayed and made the bus wait for them. The bus dropped them in the village below the chalet at a bakery where the skiers often dropped in for a coffee. The baker was a great friend of the chalet and invaluable at passing on phone messages when required. The bus was late and he could see at once from their faces that something serious had happened. Joan remembers that, without asking any questions, he simply placed a custard tart and coffee in front of her, for which she was most grateful. Then they took off their skis to walk up to the chalet and confess to Pen, who was, of course, quite cross with them for their carelessness, and told them they had half an hour to prepare for the evening's programme.

When Guides from abroad got off the bus for the first time, the baker would phone the chalet and either Joan would walk down to greet them and bring them up, or he would be asked to keep the arrivals with him for a while until someone could fetch them. Joan found some of them very interesting. There were Guides from Poland who at first could not bear to talk to anyone and were forever drawing their curtains, perhaps partly because of the conditions at home in their then Soviet-dominated country. It was fascinating watching them loosen up as their holiday progressed. Then there was a British woman with her two daughters whose husband worked for a soft-drinks company in Iran. He was still there, but the wife and daughters had been told to leave the country. They turned up at the snow-bound chalet straight from Iran wearing cotton dresses. They were Guides, and Pen was expecting them and had even managed to get some second-hand warm clothes for them from people in the village. They stayed two weeks before returning to England.

The day started very early in summer. The first task was to phone for the weather forecast at four o'clock. This was usually Joan's job, as she tended to wake up early. They would then set off after breakfast as soon as it was light, arriving at the top of the mountain in time for a second breakfast, and then go down the other side and either walk back or take a bus. Joan brought up the rear, 'picked up the bits', helping anyone who got left behind, and brought them back safely.

The parents of a Norwegian Guide in Joan's company offered their country chalet in Norway to a party of Guides for two weeks in the summer of 1971. This was to celebrate fifty years of The 1st Paddington. Eight Guides who were able to afford it, and four seniors went on the trip. They crossed from England to Norway in a fishing vessel as the only passengers and, through jumble sales and sales of work, the girls and their parents had raised enough money to hire a minibus to take with them. The Guide organisation also had a pool of money to fund such trips and as Joan had an HQ job she was in the know about how to apply. The minibus was driven by Anna Dilley (who has already been mentioned in the last chapter), an English Guide who knew some Norwegian; and Joan also had Tove Sorensen with her to help supervise the girls. As a Dane, Tove could also understand Norwegian. (When living in London Tove had been a lieutenant in the Guides and had assisted Joan with the swimming. Back in Denmark she had put Joan up whenever she came over on her swimming trips or on holiday.)

Swimming and life-saving are both important aspects of being a Guide, and all of these girls on the Norwegian trip had trained in the skills. Joan remembers being impressed by something that occurred while they were travelling. The first time they drove near water the girls were at once eager to swim. Being in the minibus with their luggage they all had their costumes and towels with them, so there was no problem, but Joan thought that ordinary girls would probably not have clamoured to go for a swim, especially as the weather was not particularly warm. Joan also remembers the deep impression left on her by a visit to a silver mine in Norway, with its narrow claustrophobic cages in which the miners were taken deep underground.

At that stage in her Guiding career Joan was also a friend of the then Chief Guide who lived alone in a grace-and-favour flat in Hampton Court Palace. As the lady became older and deafer, Joan was often summoned to escort her at receptions and other official Guide events. The old lady could hear Joan's voice quite well but would not admit to not being able to hear other people. Joan had some exciting times at Hampton Court and, because of her link with HQ, she was sometimes able to take groups of Guides with her.

When she was in her forties Joan went for two weeks as part of a Guide party to India. The first week was spent in Central India, where they visited a Guide Centre. She had always been very interested in Gandhi, and was pleased to be able to visit places connected with him including Srinagar in the far north. In 1974 Joan grasped another opportunity to visit a far-away country: Guyana. She was invited, as one of a selected group of Guide VIPs, to attend the South American country's celebrations for the 50th birthday of the formation of the Guide Movement there.

In the early 1960s a Guide company was formed at Buckingham Palace so that Princess Anne could become a Guide like her mother. This was perhaps part of an attempt to make the Princess's life as normal as possible: the Queen

once said that some of the most ordinary experiences she
was allowed to have came through the Guide movement. The
company of about twenty girls consisted mainly of daughters
of Palace staff. It was run by a Guide whom Joan had trained
in her capacity as Guide Training Adviser for England. On
behalf of Guide HQ Joan had to visit the Palace company
to see that it was running satisfactorily. The evening Guide
meeting happened to be on or around the time of St Andrew's
Day and so the saint was the theme of the meeting. Wearing
her uniform, Joan was led down many corridors to a ballroom
where she found the Guides cutting out paper figures of the
saint. Princess Anne was cutting her paper with a pen knife
and accidentally cut off the saint's legs. 'That's a pity,' said Joan,
whereupon the Princess replied: 'No, he's just kneeling.'

In the summer of 1966 Joan was the doctor for a Guide
Relay Channel Swim from Cape Gris-Nez to Sandgate,
by Folkestone. She checked health and safety aspects, made
sure the participants were warm enough and were fed and
watered, and was one of two people who regulated the
changeovers. Mac was also involved, among other things
planning the route, drawing maps and working out timings.
Selection for the six swimmers and two reserves took place in
the Serpentine in Hyde Park, where the aspiring participants
were made to swim for an hour. Training then took place in
the sea near Folkestone over several days. Two rowing boats
were anchored about a quarter of an hour's swim apart, and
the girls had to swim to and fro between them, which they
did twice a day: once in daylight and once in the dark before
midnight. Joan had to keep reminding herself that these girls
were not disabled. Before the relay could take place, the
local weather forecast had to be checked very early in the
morning. This again was Joan's job, as it had been at the chalet
in Adelboden. The relay took place on 13 August. Each of

the six girls in the team swam for an hour at a time in relay. The race started with the first swimmer walking from a fixed point on the beach down into the water to start her lap; at the finish the last swimmer had to walk up the beach to a fixed point before the race was over. Joan had to keep an eye on the swimmers to make sure they did not get into difficulties; a series of signals had been devised for communication between her and the girls. In order to leave the French coast on an outgoing tide and arrive at the English coast on an incoming one, the race had to be started at 1.30 am. After two and a half hours a fog came down, so a megaphone was used to tell the swimmers to stick close to the boat so that they could be seen. The relay was completed in 13 hours and 10 minutes, however, breaking the record for a junior female cross-Channel swim. By demonstrating the principles of courage and concentration, the achievement helped to put Guiding on the map.

Encouraged by this success Joan and Mac organised a Channel relay for disabled swimmers at the end of August 1970. Four men, two women and two reserves were selected at a session in the Serpentine and swam the race from Cape Gris-Nez to Sandgate; all but one, a man who had lost a leg, were polio victims. The procedures for the race were the same except that some of the swimmers had to be lowered into the water by means of a hoist. The last lap was swum by the youngest swimmer, a sixteen-year-old who, in order to reach the point up on the beach which marked the finishing line, had to crawl on her hands and knees up the rough, pebbly shore. Joan was quite concerned that she would graze her skin. The race was achieved in 14 hours and 1 minute. It happened to be the fastest time for a Channel relay swim in the whole of 1970, partly because the sea conditions had been so poor throughout that summer.

In 1966, at Porchester Swimming Baths near Notting Hill, the County Commissioner for N.W. London, Mrs Sheila Constantinide, handed Joan the Beaver Award for outstanding service to the Guide movement over thirty years. This is the second-highest award in the Guides after the Silver Fish. The Golden Fish is higher than the Silver but has only ever been awarded to World Chief Guide Lady Olave Baden-Powell. Joan still regularly attends Guide HQ in her capacity as Vice-President of the International Committee, having been Chairman and then President for several years.

7. Africa

For most of 1963 Joan worked voluntarily in Southern Africa. As Guide Training Adviser for England she knew that training jobs were available abroad. She was regularly in touch with an African Guide, Kgopodiso Mokama, whom she had trained in England and who had returned to Botswana (and later became Chief Commissioner of Guides in Botswana), and through her she found out about a post which was suddenly vacant because the person due to take it on had died unexpectedly. Joan let her flat and took a year off from her job as a doctor in Kensington. The Borough agreed to put it on hold, especially as Joan would be working with Africans: the Council's work, after all, was often with minority ethnic groups.

Joan's task that year was to prepare the Girl Guide movements in Basutoland, Bechuanaland and Swaziland for those countries' independence from Britain in the late sixties, and therefore their Guide movements' independence of Britain and the Republic of South Africa (RSA). Basutoland, an enclave surrounded by the RSA, was a Crown colony, which gained independence in 1966, becoming the Kingdom of Lesotho. Bechuanaland, bordered by RSA to the south and southeast, was a British protectorate that also gained independence in 1966, becoming the Republic of Botswana. Swaziland, bordered by RSA to the north, south and west, was also a British protectorate until its independence in 1968. In 1962 the Guide companies of these three territories were under the umbrella of the Girl Guide organisation of RSA. The organisation in Britain had now decided that the companies of the territories needed to stand on their own feet. (To avoid confusion these territories will from now on be referred to by their modern names, rather than their names at the time.)

Joan left England for Johannesburg just after Christmas 1962, at the beginning of the famously cold winter. Despite the extreme temperatures planes were still taking off from Heathrow Airport, but Joan, who had never flown in a jet airliner before, was amazed at how the plane took off so fast and at such a steep angle. Even more surprising and somewhat alarming was the fact that after the plane levelled out it suddenly did another fast climb, levelled out again and then repeated these manoeuvres yet again. By this time Joan was convinced they were going to crash. The other passengers sat silently with mouths open, but nothing untoward happened after that. (The explanation is probably that, with several levels of airspace monitored for traffic, the pilot was at first only cleared to a certain height, then subsequently cleared to higher levels.) At Johannesburg Joan was picked up and driven to a hotel. The unaccustomed heat made her feel quite ill. Sitting in her hotel room she suddenly remembered that one should take salt in hot countries. She had none with her, but she did have Marmite and so started regularly taking the odd teaspoonful. It was a Sunday, so she went to a service in the cathedral.

Joan's mission was to teach the African Guide officials how they could be independent of any help from white South African officials, although they had always been very useful. The Africans were to become members in their own right and had to learn how to manage their own finances too, earning their own money. This they were able to do in small ways by cleaning in the missions, for example. Joan also brought some money from England to start them off, with strict instructions to give it to the right people and also *not* to give it to the South Africans. The South African officials could not imagine how the black Africans could possibly manage on their own and so Joan had to instruct them too. Over years the three territories did achieve their independence from the South Africans, and each eventually had its own right to vote on the World Guide committees. With apartheid so entrenched at the time, the Africans were amazed at a white woman coming to work with them. One of Joan's opposite numbers in the Scouts came out to southern Africa on the same sort of mission, but only stayed for six weeks – Joan thinks the Guides tend to take things more seriously.

From Johannesburg Joan had to visit the territories, each one twice and for about six weeks at a time, travelling by train and on arrival driving or being driven between locations, returning to Johannesburg between each six-week visit. Her stays in Johannesburg were a welcome time for Joan – to have her hair cut, have baths and other such luxuries. The South African commissioners regulated her activities and entertained her each time she returned to the capital. They were fascinated by the idea of a white woman working with black Africans. Each time she returned they would ask: 'What have you done now?'. They were amazed by the hardships she was prepared to endure, such as only having one meal a day, in the middle of the day, and nothing before bedtime. Out in the territories she often stayed in camps when doing the training, but in between was also accommodated at missions, in monasteries or nunneries or, best of all, in hospitals, where she was with people with whom she had a lot in common.

Monasteries and nunneries were often together on one site, although the men and women were kept separate. Joan slept in the nunnery but was allowed to eat with the monks, who had better food. Joan still has friends who were sister tutors (senior sisters who trained the nurses) at the mission hospitals where she stayed, many of them from Scotland, like

Dr David Livingstone. This was Livingstone country and his name often cropped up, and houses where he had stayed were sometimes pointed out to her: they were by now just piles of stones.

As far as the safety of British medical staff and government servants was concerned, Joan knew that if the territory where they were was to be invaded from the north or if there were any other kind of violence, the only advice was to make their way to the coast where the British Navy would pick them up. In the sixties, which was not so long after rebellions such as the Mau Mau in Kenya, unrest was always a possibility. The police chief in one area Joan visited had records of the victims of similar uprisings, and, to her horror, she saw that most of the known dead were Christians. Perhaps knowing that she was a doctor the policeman solemnly made Joan look at the gruesome details of their torture and deaths. As it happened, Joan was also able to visit Kenya, including the game reserves, while she was in Africa in 1963. (She was able to visit again when she flew out at the end of 1980 for a New Year's holiday staying with friends. This was the family whose mother and daughters had turned up in their cotton dresses at the chalet at Adelboden, having had to leave the father behind in Iran. His company later moved him to Nairobi where his family were able to join him again. Joan had made such good friends with the mother and daughters that they had kept in touch. Unfortunately, her main memory of that holiday in Nairobi was of a family barbecue in the garden on New Year's Eve. Suddenly there was a huge explosion. Joan said: 'That was a bomb.' It was the bomb which blew up the Norfolk Hotel.)

The Dulverton Trust, a grant-making organisation that gives money to UK-registered charities, paid for the vehicles in each territory, including a jeep that Joan used in Botswana (she had had to learn how to drive one before leaving

England). Bizarrely, she was provided with a quite unsuitable Mini in Swaziland and another standard car in Lesotho, both of which territories were very mountainous: how she longed for her jeep. She always travelled first class on trains, but if any of her trainees were on the train too they had to sit in the carriages for blacks only. Knowing that she was on the train though they could not resist coming to see her in first class, their excuse being that they wanted to check that she was all right; but this caused no end of trouble with the train officials and so Joan always tried to stop them from staying. On station platforms, blacks and whites were separated too, and Joan, desperate to find a seat anywhere in the heat, often unwittingly sat on benches for blacks only.

Travel by train was often by night. Once she was going to Molepolole, the largest village in Botswana, where she was due to stay at the Scottish Livingstone Hospital. She was to be met at the station. She arrived at midnight, but there was no one there. There was no seat so she sat on her luggage on the platform in some despair, especially since it was pitch black and she could hear a lion roaring in the distance. Eventually she saw two gleaming white points coming towards her: they were the whites of the eyes of an African official who told her she could not be collected until the morning and took her to a wooden shed to sleep. It was overrun with rats, so she sat on top of her luggage all night, but this did not prevent beetles from crawling over her feet all night. The next morning someone from the hospital arrived in a lorry to collect her, full of apologies. The hospital had had to deal with an accident and no one had been free. Joan came to love this hospital at Molepolole and she went back to stay as often as she could: it became a kind of second home.

Joan did not teach the Girl Guides but their teachers and nurses: she was training them to be trainers. Her instructing was done mainly at weekends: during the week the trainees were at work, and evenings were so dark that they would only have been able to sit round a camp fire, although very occasionally they worked by candlelight. During the week she could rest, sightsee and travel around the territory. At about six the sun went down and camp fires were lit, using chopped-down trees, even though there was a great shortage. Joan sometimes found the fires quite frightening and thought she might get burnt. The largest fires were lit on Saturday nights and there was much singing and dancing by the whole village. Plays were also acted out, and some of the songs were Guide songs. When Joan returned to England she wondered what she would find to do on Saturday nights, she had become so used to the ritual.

Although hot by day, the nights could be very cold, and Joan was very glad when, quite early on, the Africans presented her, amid great ceremony, with a large blanket. Someone had apparently simply taken the best they could find from some unfortunate African and given it to her. She did not know if it had been 'paid' for. It seemed to be made of 'shoddy', that is wool waste or clippings. Joan used it in the evenings and to supplement her sleeping bag. In the end it was so worn out that she had to throw it away. Her entire wardrobe in Africa consisted of three summer dresses, a pair of trousers, an anorak and two medium-thick jumpers; she had been advised not to take one thick and one thin, wearing the medium two in layers was quite sufficient. She never went barefoot because of snakes, but wore sandals most of the time.

If the companies were to become independent, then their Brownies' and Guides' tests had to be adapted to their lifestyle and culture. For example, one of the usual Brownie tests was washing up, but the Africans all ate by hand from a single dish which was then thrown into the sand. This was their 'washing up'. So Joan had to think up something else for them to do, such as how to tie a parcel. The Africans were wonderful at tying knots because of all the weaving they did. It tended to be the Brownie tests, in fact, that were least suitable. Cleaning shoes was another standard test but most of the Africans had no shoes, so they had to clean the missionaries' shoes, which was rather artificial. The Scouts tended to go in for cleaning the missionaries' shoes more and, despite the heat, would sometimes walk around triumphantly with clean shoes tied around their necks. The Guide tests were, on the whole, more suitable for the Africans. They loved Kim's Game (derived from Kipling's novel *Kim*) which involves looking at a number of objects laid out and then trying to remember them after they have been covered up. The African's memories tended to be much better than Westerners' because most had no books to supplement their memories. The Guide teachers found it all very exciting, especially when Joan gave them a compass. She did this in Botswana, her first territory, bleak and empty, situated as it is in the Kalahari Desert. Just how she managed to explain how a compass works she no longer remembers, but it was certainly very difficult. She also took them on a trek 3,000 feet up a local mountain – something which her pupils would never have considered doing – and they were quite entranced by the view and greatly excited at seeing the one train of the day chugging through the landscape. It had taken a lot of persuading to get them to trek in the first place as they were very afraid of encountering wild animals, which they did not, of course, since animals tend to keep well away from humans. In fact, Joan had to bribe them: they would not be allowed to eat any of the picnic until they got to the top of the mountain.

Joan also had the opportunity to enrol Guides and adult Guiders from time to time. The Guides wore nothing from the waist up until they were about fourteen, but they would at least wear the tie onto which the badge was pinned on enrolment. The badge is a trefoil symbolising the three Guide promises. Traditionally it is pinned on with the right hand, while the left hand is offered to be shaken – Guides shake hands with the left. But this will not do for Africans, who, for reasons of hygiene, cannot shake with their 'toileting' hand. Eventually all Girl Guides wore shirts as everyone's clothes became more westernised. The missionaries had arrived wearing long white garments, which African women eventually copied, but they tended to wear black rather than white.

Joan found it a great privilege to work in a part of the world where Baden-Powell had devised the concept and principles of the Boy Scouts. As an officer in the Boer War he had tried many ways of disciplining the Africans under his command. Joan now understood why things like fire-lighting, knotting and teaching about other countries were so important in the Scouts and Guides. There was a large Christian missionary presence there, mainly Roman Catholics whom the Africans loved because of all the brightly-coloured garments and trappings, and the many candles. The Catholics ran the richest and best-organised missions, with stone buildings, unlike the Anglicans, the 'poor relations' who were housed in mud huts. There were also Non-Conformists such as the Dutch Reformed, German Lutherans, Baptists, Methodists and the Swiss Calvinists. The Non-Conformists, especially the Dutch, the 'conquerors' of South Africa, were very strict and severe.

Joan quite often undertook activities with the missionaries' children. Those aged seven and over were all at boarding school, but there were plenty of under-sevens who were bored much of the time and they even joined in the training sessions. If it was still daylight at the end of a session, the children might ask Joan to go with them to the village to see something they had heard about; they were not allowed to go alone. The sights they were curious to see might be a dead dog or wooden coffins being made. Joan remembers one glorious day when a boy and girl, children of Anglican missionaries, persuaded her to walk with them along the course of a dried-up river, something they had wanted to do for a while. They took a picnic and were to be picked up by car at the end. They were protected from the sun by over-hanging trees. Joan suddenly remembered that snakes such as the deadly mamba might be about, and was frightened of treading on one. The children noticed that she was walking somewhat gingerly and asked her why. She replied: 'Snakes' to which they replied: 'Overhead, silly!': the mambas hung around in trees. But that trek proved not to have been without danger, for Joan picked up tick-bite fever and within a couple of days felt as if she had the most appalling 'flu, with a sensitive area on her stomach, the site of the bite. When the symptoms came on she was on a lorry being driven to a Dutch-Reformed mission for a training weekend. It was one of the few occasions when she was not doing the driving herself. She was sitting next to the driver, with her head lolling and he asked her if she was ill. 'I don't feel well,' she replied, whereupon he said: 'I feel ill too'. She heard later that he had tuberculosis. At the mission, where the regime was so strict that even heating water was a forbidden luxury, she was shown no sympathy and had to work the full weekend, despite her fever. Fortunately she was able to recover somewhat during the following days when she was not training. She had no medication but drank plenty of water. Even so, it took her about a month to get completely well. Fortunately this was the only time Joan was really ill during her time in Africa.

Joan loved staying at hospitals with people in her profession. She could discuss problems she had encountered at the camps and how they might be solved. She was amazed at the distances people travelled on foot to the hospital, sometimes for as long as six weeks, dragging a sick relative all the way on a kind of sled. By the time they arrived, the patient was usually half dead, if not completely. Joan was keen to visit a leper colony, but no one wanted her to. By chance she found out that the nursing officer in charge of a colony high in the mountains had been at Joan's boarding school, Hunmanby Hall, so the gates were, after all, opened to her. She spent about two hours at the colony, which consisted of a clinic and individual mud huts where the patients lived alone or with family. She was glad that they appeared to be well cared for.

Sometimes Joan was able to be useful to the hospitals. In Botswana, the Scottish Livingstone Hospital in Molepolole served huge areas of the Kalahari Desert. They would send out medical teams, including a doctor, along set routes to the medical centres, the journey taking about three days there and three days back with a day spent there in between. They visited each centre every six weeks, and it was essential that they did not miss a visit. People knew that Joan was a doctor although she was not in Africa in that capacity and when many of the hospital doctors fell ill at the same time Joan went on one of these treks as a doctor, which she found very exciting. Her nurse for that week was Marion Peter, a Scottish sister tutor (now back in Scotland and still in touch with Joan).

They travelled over the desert by lorry accompanied by several men, including two white South African medical students who turned out to be very useful, reminding Joan of the two who had helped in the Bethnal Green disaster. Their destination was a mission: a collection of mud huts including a church. As Joan got off the lorry there she was given a present of a live hen – complete with fleas. This was the most precious present that the Africans could give: they did not have much else. The next thing that happened was that another African came with great ceremony and wrung its neck right in front of her, and an hour or so later Joan was eating it. This was to be the first of many times that this ritual was performed in her honour. The medical party stayed in the mission, a long mud hut on stone foundations with palm leaves as a roof, with the women at one end and men at the other. Joan and Marion were put in the centre with their sleeping bags, between the two groups.

After the welcome came a church service. Hymns were only rarely in English, normally they were sung in the local language. Joan was fascinated by the dramatic way that the Bible stories were acted out for the congregation. The most exciting, Joan remembers, was the enactment of the paralysed man being lowered through a roof for Jesus to heal him (Mark, Chapter 2). They tied a man to a flimsy-looking wooden stretcher and climbed precariously up a tree with it to lower it for the healing. After the service the African nurse in charge of the medical centre would list all the medical work that was needed. The hospital team had very limited quantities of medicine. The first patient they saw was a very sick baby who seemed to have meningitis, so there was almost no hope, but after conferring with Marion, Joan felt they should try to save it. They would treat the infant as best they could with antibiotics and, if in the morning its condition was improved or no worse, they would take the child back with them to the hospital, which was its only chance of survival. Joan had a restless night agonising about the child, who was apparently much loved and very precious to its family. Mothers of such children always had complete trust in white doctors and were only too glad for them to take the child to the hospital. This is what was done in this case, Joan nursing the baby on the entire journey. The child lived and was taken back to the village on the team's next visit. The hospital's reputation depended on decisions like these. Another task for the visiting team was to inspect everything and leave instructions on what needed doing before their next visit. More often than not these were ignored, however. It was often a similar story when it came to instructing the Guide trainees.

Joan always tried to go to church on a Sunday even though she could not understand what was being said, and she never came across a communion service. Although she always stressed that she was not in Africa as a doctor, the word would get around, and when she came out of church, usually accompanied by a government official, there might be half a dozen people wanting medical attention. But she only had enough medication on her for her own needs, mainly snake-bite anti-venom, so they just had to turn and walk away. Very occasionally Joan would take a look at ill people in camp; in Botswana she often had Marion with her who knew more about the kind of illnesses the people would have – and also knew that they had no remedies for them. At other times when Marion was not with her, another well-informed person might step forward to help her, which she desperately needed. She says she made many mistakes and was very glad to get back to base every six weeks where she could take advice.

Joan got to know Seretse Khama, who became the first President of Botswana and was knighted by the Queen when the country became independent. As a child he had become King of the protectorate, with his uncle as regent. He came to England to study law and was training to be a barrister in the Inner Temple in 1947 when he met Ruth Williams, an

Englishwoman working for Lloyd's of London. After a year of courtship they wanted to be married but South Africa's strict apartheid laws did not allow mixed marriages, and Britain respected this for diplomatic reasons, which was a problem. The Botswanan government also declared that they should not marry. The couple were not living together, but wanted to legalise their relationship and had arranged to marry at St Mary Abbots Church, Kensington. When they arrived for the ceremony the Bishop of Kensington, Henry Campbell, who had been told by the British government not to allow the ceremony to take place, slammed the church door in their faces in a dramatic gesture. The door-slamming incident was hushed up and eventually the couple managed a secret marriage up the road at St George's Church, Campden Hill, which at the time was still a parish church in its own right and not yet merged with St Mary Abbots.

As a respected visitor to southern Africa Joan was often a guest of important people. By 1963 Seretse was an eminent politician, and Ruth had been accepted by the people, indeed was very popular. They had four children: the eldest was in the army, a twelve-year-old girl was at boarding school and the naughty six-year-old boy-and-girl twins were at home; Joan says 'they climbed the curtains', and she thinks it is because they had to be so restrained a lot of the time. Joan would be driven around in Seretse's grand car, and the twins would often accompany her; they came to the training sessions, even candlelit ones in the evenings, and became experts in knotting and other such skills that were completely new to them; and they were completely fascinated by a compass.

Anyone from a place like Botswana who was able to go to England to study, by definition had to come from the upper stratum of society and was expected to take on important work when they returned to their home country. Knowing

Kgopodiso well (whom she had first trained in England) was a great help to Joan, as was her husband Moleleki Mokama, Attorney General of Botswana. He had met his wife at the Methodist Youth Club when he was studying law in London and she was training to be a teacher. It was there that they decided to get married, and there was a big fuss about this wedding too, despite this not being a mixed marriage: in Africa there would have been an exchange of cattle, among other ceremonies, and they were told they must be married in Botswana. However, they did marry in London. Joan was a guest at the wedding, and the bride was married from Phyl Macmillan's home (Phyl being the wife of swimming therapist Mac). Joan already knew them because she was training Kgopodiso as a Guide trainer. Phyl was a Guide too and the Macmillans had had Kgopodiso lodging in their house where she had become like a daughter to them.

Joan also got to know Quett Masire, who was later President of Botswana (1980–1998). Seretse, Moleleki and Quett all attended university in South Africa together and remained great friends. Joan remembers one day driving in the desert with the Mokamas where they were to meet Quett and the Khamas. The three men were delighted to see each other and talk politics, and all settled down for a picnic. Finally Kgopodiso stood up and said with some dignity: 'Gentlemen, we are not here to run the country but to organise the Guide movement. Get back in your cars and go.' All three men came quite regularly to England on business in later years, and Joan often saw them if they passed through London.

Joan had brought a lot of equipment from England to give to the Guides: compasses, coloured cord for knotting, crayons, paper. She had to keep a sharp eye out because the Africans would try to steal them whenever they could. She taught the Guide laws, but then there was thrift. Trying to teach thrift to people who had nothing in the first place was not easy: to them thrift was getting a free ride on a lorry instead of paying the usual few pennies. Once in camp when everyone was sitting in the usual horseshoe having their midday meal, Joan found herself in the middle with local dignitaries who were sometimes invited. She had to give a short talk first, and on this occasion she had chosen the subject of thrift. When Joan's helping was being offered to her, mindful to be thrifty, she asked for a very small portion, at which her plate was taken away and the local princess received a huge helping. Unfortunately Joan's plate was not returned and she missed the one meal of the day altogether. This was not the only time this sort of thing happened, and she was lucky if she even got a glass of water. Fortunately, when she went back to base the South Africans always gave her a lot of fruit to supplement her diet, so when the midday meal went missing she could fall back on that.

Being at midday, the meal had to be taken under cover from the sun. It consisted solely of a kind of porridge made of mealie (maize or millet) which, although made more palatable by sugar and salt, Joan hated, as indeed she hates porridge. On one occasion the meal had been made when it was discovered that there was no sugar or salt left in camp to put in it, so all the food was thrown away. Joan was horrified and told Kgopodiso that the people could not go without food for a whole day. As it happened, Joan had some vegetables which some tradespeople had given her as a present, so she told Kgopodiso to carry on with the training without her while she prepared the vegetables for everyone. It was fortunate that this was her last day in that camp, for when she told the South Africans in Johannesburg about it they said that, had she stayed longer, she would have been expected to prepare vegetables for everyone every day: in this society, once you started something you were stuck with it.

Joan was fascinated by the way the Africans ate: they would make a round ball of the food and pop it in their mouths. Joan had been told to take with her one bowl, a plate, a large spoon, a small spoon, and knife and fork. These she kept in a bag. If the Africans could possibly steal any of them they did: they longed to try eating with cutlery. At her very last camp she gave all her cutlery away since she did not wish to take it back with her. When an African woman served food she would, of course, only use her clean right hand. But she kept her left hand visible by resting it on the inside of her right elbow. This was so that people could see that she was not holding a knife behind her back.

Occasionally, when Joan was invited to lunch at a dignitary's house, some of the African commissioners were invited with her. There they could not eat with their hands, the tables were laid for a four-course meal with a great selection of cutlery at each place. While the Africans watched Joan carefully to see the order in which she used her forks and spoons, the African servants were watching to see if she or her black companions made a mistake – something they could laugh about afterwards, no doubt. Joan tried her hardest to get it right as it was quite a responsibility.

The camps where Joan stayed were never in the bush but in the grounds of a large building such as a hospital or a government house. The Africans were used to camping, and loved being given tents, but sometimes the ridge tents provided came without poles, so they simply cut down a tree, and trees, as already mentioned, were in short supply. Joan can remember a scene where tents were being pitched, and among the bustle and activity a woman calmly sat breast-feeding her baby. On her very first night in camp Joan insisted on sleeping on the ground. The Africans were not at all happy about this – she was far too important. The next morning she found she had been lying on a snake (by now dead), so she was persuaded to use a camp bed after all. Sometimes she slept with the Africans in their mud huts; then she was on the hard floor. The only furniture in the huts were tea chests or double containers which could be used as shelves.

Swaziland was the second territory Joan visited. Here the terrain and the people were quite different. The landscape was of magnificent rounded mountains of granite. The Swazis loved dressing up in colourful garments and putting clay and feathers in their hair. They were a much more laid-back people because they had food in plenty: the climate was perfect for growing many fruits and vegetables. If there was trouble between tribes they retreated into caves with their cattle until it was over. Joan, being a caver, made sure that she saw inside one of these. She could see that the people seemed in essence to live just like ancient cavemen. She found the people very easy-going but with less drive than the Botswanans. They simply did not want to work if they could help it, so she found them quite difficult to train.

When she moved on to cooler Lesotho the landscape and the people were different again. Here too were mountains, but this time they were pointed, and the people were bright and keen, working hard – if they were minded to. She found the Basotho, as the people of Lesotho are called, the hardest of the three peoples to deal with, mainly because they were less frank and outspoken. Lesotho seemed to Joan the most permanent and sophisticated of the three territories, with better buildings, schools and hospitals. Here she was expected to go and talk to a school if she was in the area, and having most weekdays free, this was quite possible. Whenever there was a problem, the Basotho blamed the tokoloshe, the evil sprite feared by most southern African tribes. To her consternation Joan found herself agreeing after a while and realised she was getting indoctrinated. The sooner she left this territory the better, she thought. She was glad that she had started off in Botswana where she had had a chance to see how things could be worked out.

It was frustrating never being able to swim while in Africa, the danger of catching bilharzia – or 'swimmer's itch', a parasitic disease that can lead to permanent ill health – was far too great, but in Swaziland and Lesotho Joan had a chance to satisfy her passion for rock climbing. This had to be fitted into an afternoon before sundown because it was only in the afternoons that the men who would accompany her could get time off work. She discovered the odd government servant who loved climbing and wanted a companion, so she always had one such man with her. They would get into his car and drive to the mountains, she wearing her trousers and a pair of gym shoes (which were in ribbons by the end of her stay), and he providing the ropes. She remembers one quite frightening climb which involved crawling and partly wriggling on their stomachs along a narrow ledge with a huge drop to one side, only to find that the way was blocked so that they had to wriggle all the way back, feet first, as there was no room to turn round. This was achieved with much difficulty. Luckily Joan only ever suffered the odd graze on these climbing jaunts.

Joan was never supposed to travel alone, by car or on a train, but as it turned out she was often alone. She was warned never to stop to pick anyone up and was quite determined to stick to this advice until one day when she relented. She was driving in Swaziland and saw an old, decrepit woman by the road. When she stopped to pick her up the old woman did not seem to mind at all where she was going, just anywhere.

Joan suddenly noticed that the woman had a hen in her lap whereupon the woman started trying to give it to her as a present, she was so grateful. Joan kept refusing it, of course, and had a job keeping the steering wheel steady while beating off the attempts of the women to press the hen into her lap. At other times she would see an incident by the road, but she knew that it would be madness to stop. Some of the lorries she travelled in had cabins with a bed across the back, which was quite comfortable and also a good vantage point for watching wildlife, such as ostriches, from the back of the vehicle. On long lorry journeys, comfort stops were discreetly achieved by Joan suggesting that the driver go on one side of the lorry while she went on the other. (For African women this was less awkward: they wore no underwear under their long black robes, and managed the procedure standing up.)

Joan found the question of religion in southern Africa very interesting. There was no set religion anywhere: the people had witch doctors who seemed omnipotent, and they might believe in devils like the tokoloshe, but there was no real creed. Thus they accepted Christianity quite happily, but in a way that suited their own particular culture. The person taking a service would walk around the village beforehand with two sticks tied together to form a cross, and gather the congregation. Worship was conducted in the open air, in a mud hut, or a stone building if it was Roman Catholic. The Non-Conformist buildings varied but were usually better than the Anglicans' (although the latter's hospitals compared quite favourably with the Non-Conformists'). In general it was hoped that the Africans would take over the running of the churches from the missionaries. One Roman Catholic church's arrangements seemed to Joan to be utterly Christian: an African was appointed as priest while the European missionary stayed on merely as his assistant. On the whole, the Catholics seemed better than the other denominations at handing over.

All Christian denominations had their own Guide companies, so there were Roman Catholic Guides, Anglican Guides and Non-Conformist Guides. Joan declared that she was there for all of them. The Africans could not understand why she would not only deal with the Anglican Guides. But she was not there for religion. One evening, when she was training by candlelight, she explained that the Guides and Scouts in England were one movement, irrespective of religion. Suddenly something seemed to dawn on her listeners: 'So you're all heathen!' one of them cried, the others seeming to agree. Quite a different mindset from that of the Europeans.

Joan flew back to England from Johannesburg on 22 November 1963. There was to be one refuelling stopover on the way. During the first flight the captain announced to the passengers that President Kennedy had been shot but that it was not known if he was still alive. There were several Americans on board who became very upset and agitated. Alcohol being very cheap in South Africa they seemed to have brought quite a lot of it on board and proceeded to drink at an alarming rate. During the stopover it was then announced that the President had died. On the second flight the Americans drank even more despite the stewardesses' attempts to stop them. They became extremely rowdy and even violent, which was very alarming for the other passengers, and some were subsequently arrested at Heathrow Airport. The people who came to meet Joan, and later her mother, were amazed that she had already heard the dramatic news.

It was an extraordinary end to an exhausting year. Joan was very gratified that her work had its effect and the African Guides eventually got their independence. She says that the Guide movement has always had a soft spot for the Africans.

8. The Pilgrim

Although brought up as a Methodist, Joan quite early on became fascinated by the Anglican Church: its buildings, forms of service and rituals. She is now a faithful Anglican and has attended St Mary Abbots Church, Kensington High Street, for at least thirty years, from when she moved into the area. She regularly attends the 9.30 Sunday-morning service, the monthly Taizé and healing services, and any special extra services such as the Patronal Festival. Despite finding walking about quite painful for her knees these days, from years of running down mountainsides ('I was really quite good at that!') she is always willing to help where she can. She regularly prepares the refreshments for the Friday lunchtime recitals by students from the Royal College of Music and she belongs to the handicraft group that recycles Christmas cards and makes quilts and other items for the church bazaar. Most weeks she does a gardening job for the Vicarage alongside the employed gardeners who are happy to let her weed and trim. In her flat once a month she hosts a book club supervised by the Revd Rob Marshall. Father Rob is now an honorary priest at St Mary Abbots and well known for his BBC Radio 4 'Thought for the day' talks on Saturday mornings. He has become a good friend. Joan's church activities are not limited to St Mary Abbots, however: she also belongs to the Luncheon Club at St George's Church, on top of Campden Hill, where she makes a point of talking to the sixth-form pupils from Holland Park School who serve the food as volunteers on a rota basis. One of them told her that it was often months before they got a turn at it. Recently Joan has been attending the nine o'clock 'Night Prayer' at St Philip's Church, Earls Court Road, just a few yards from her flat. She finds this reflective, prayerful, 20-minute candlelit service the perfect, peaceful ending to a Sunday.

Recently there has been a new slant to her religious life: she has been on seven pilgrimages in fifteen years. The first, in 1995, was to the Holy Land, led by the then Bishop of London, David Hope, and Father Rob. She says that if she had known that there would be about 200 people in the party she would not have gone. The pilgrims filled four or five coaches; among them were the Revd Ian Robson, then Vicar of St Mary Abbots, and his wife Liz. Joan's favourite place in the Holy Land was the Sea of Galilee which she felt must still look largely as it did to Jesus – she could just imagine the fishing boats pushing out from the little beaches. The service on a boat in the middle of the sea with the engines turned off was very moving. Breaking the silence, however, was occasional gunfire, and during the whole pilgrimage Joan found the armed military presence, the tension and the general atmosphere of conflict, especially in Jerusalem, very disturbing. Nazareth was interesting, but Joan was very disappointed by Bethlehem, a characterless fortified town – even more so now, by all accounts – with the Church of the Nativity so elaborately decorated that she could not imagine Jesus being born there. The effect of Christ seemed also very diluted in the Jerusalem churches, and unfortunately, as it happened, the pilgrims were conducted along the Stations of the Cross in the city's streets in the pouring autumn rain.

One quite exciting event took place in Jerusalem while Joan was there. She was lying in her hotel bed early one morning when the room started to shake violently. She knew that this was an earth tremor from her many experiences of them in Japan. She was quite high up in the building, there were no instructions on the door about procedures during earthquakes, and she wondered if she should slip under the bed. While she was thinking about it the tremor stopped so she stayed where she was. At breakfast everyone had a story to tell.

Another place that Joan felt had altered little since Jesus' time was Mount Tabor, on which his Transfiguration is thought to have taken place. The pilgrims were taken up in a fleet of taxis, since the coaches were too large for the many tight hairpin bends. On the summit were a church and a monastery, which Joan found very impressive, and Bishop David Hope's service in the church was wonderful. Joan was longing to stretch her legs afterwards and asked if she could walk down the mountain instead of going by taxi, but she was firmly told that this would take far too long: for once her knees were spared. Swimming, or rather floating, in the Dead Sea was also a great experience. Joan knew that the water was supposed to be so salty that you could not sink, but until she got there she did not quite believe it. She also visited the flat-topped mountain of Masada, nearby to the west. Herod the Great had had a three-tiered villa built on the top, along with many store-houses and huge water cisterns that could hold vast amounts of water ingeniously captured during flash floods. Here, after the Roman sacking of Jerusalem in 70 AD, a group of Jewish Zealots and their families had held out under siege for three years, until the Romans had painstakingly built a long ramp to the top of the mountain, only to find that the people they had hoped to capture for slaves had almost all committed suicide. The buildings are all ruins now, but Joan was completely fascinated, walking around such a relatively small place, with sheer drops of over 1,000 feet on all sides, imagining how 960 men, women and children and their livestock could have survived here for three years.

Joan's second pilgrimage was to Italy: Padua, Verona and Venice. This was in 2002 and led by the Bishop of Kensington,

Michael Colclough, accompanied by his wife, Cynthia. Joan always found the Bishop a good teacher: he explained things simply but well, and although this was largely a sightseeing trip, there were always plenty of church services arranged. One was in the Church of St Anthony in Padua, the Portuguese St Anthony being Padua's patron saint, as well as Italy's. Joan could not help remembering a friend who was always praying to St Anthony to help her find things she had lost – many people invoke him for this particular task. The group consisted only of around twelve pilgrims and two other priests. Joan says that on these journeys the 'singles' tended to get together, and it was on this pilgrimage that she got to know Carys Wynne (on this occasion without her husband Willoughby) who was a life and soul of Kensington society until her premature death in 2009. Also with them was Michael Miller, a Scouter and a great friend of Joan's, having been introduced to her by the Bishop some time before. He has since been ordained and is now Vicar of St Thomas Kensal Town. This was Joan's first visit to Italy, which she found a fascinating country. In Venice she was shocked that St Mark's Square was regularly flooded so that pedestrians were often wading ankle-deep in sea water sometimes twice in one day. The thought of the damage being done to that beautiful city did not bear thinking about.

The third pilgrimage was also led by Bishop Michael and was in Turkey in the autumn of 2003, commencing in Smyrna and called 'A Voyage with St Paul. A Visit to the Seven Churches of Asia'. The pilgrims travelled by coach for a week as far as Ephesus. Joan found the huge ancient amphitheatres incredibly impressive. Near the start of their overland journey they also visited the remains of an ancient centre of healing that had a long tunnel along which mentally ill patients could take exercise, but with no way out. This seemed very cruel, but Joan noted with interest that water was used a lot for healing at these centres – right up her street.

In St Paul's time, Ephesus was on the coast. Now it is inland, so the pilgrims were taken by coach to the coast where they boarded a small boat and cruised along the coast for another week. One of the stops was Iassos, an ancient ruined Carian city, now just a fishing village called Kiyikislak. It was full of fascinating archaeology. From there the pilgrims were taken up a mountain by coach to Labranda, a city famous for its Temple of Zeus as well as many other ruins. Joan found this the most interesting place she visited on land; she went off and explored on her own and found that there were even ancient domestic areas among the ruins. The party ate a picnic up there, but soon they were being hurried back down to the harbour because quite visible from the mountain top was a distant storm inland; they could see clouds of swirling dust and objects being hurled into the air. Yet the storm took its time coming: it was not until about four the next morning that the terrible gale and thunderstorm were upon them and the boat crew started rushing around, moving the boat out from the harbour where it would be safer from the land-based storm. They then rode at anchor for several hours until the storm had passed. Later in the day when the sun was shining and the sea looked inviting, the Bishop suggested a swim from the anchored boat. Once in their costumes, the pilgrims began to look a bit doubtful, so the Bishop decided to set an example by taking the plunge. He was not a secure swimmer and the cold water and its unexpected depth were quite a shock. Joan was alarmed to see him apparently in difficulties. She leapt in without a moment's thought and swam up to him. At first he tried to hold on to her but she shouted straight into his face: 'Now, you must do *exactly* as I say!' She told him to roll on to his back, stop moving and do absolutely nothing. He knew that Joan worked with swimmers and was obedience itself, and she was able to pull him to the steps into the boat. Afterwards he was quite matter of fact, although he thanked her, of course, and after Joan had encouraged others to come into the sea with her, he went back in again for a bit of a swim round. Afterwards they drank some wine to celebrate and to steady their nerves, perhaps. It turned out to be the communion wine.

Another 'single' on this pilgrimage was Ailsie Corbell, stalwart parishioner of St Mary Abbots, who became a great friend to Joan; sadly she had just lost her husband and had needed a lot of persuading to come at all. She and Joan shared a cabin, and the Bishop recounts that he, his wife and the two ladies would have little cocktail sessions before dinner each evening: he and Cynthia would creep into their cabin, the Bishop bearing a bottle of whisky for himself while Joan and Ailsie enjoyed their brandy (and Cynthia abstained).

The last stop on the coast was Bodrum, a holiday resort, but also very interesting historically. From there they flew to Istanbul where they spent two or three days. Joan's main impressions of Istanbul were the mosques, museums and the difficulty in crossing roads. Ailsie proved very useful when shopping in the bazaars of Istanbul: an expert haggler who led the stallholders to believe that Joan was a poor old woman with very little money, she managed to get her a waistcoat she wanted – at a knocked-down price of £5, Joan all the while struggling to control a fit of laughter.

The fourth pilgrimage, again led by Bishop Michael, was 'The Saints of the North'. This was a two-week coach trip. Joan says that had she known it would be by coach she would not have gone. However, she found travelling across the north of England and the west of Scotland, parts of which she knew well, was very interesting: she was now following a long route through continuously and seeing how the places related geographically. She had never before realised the extent of the North when she had lived there. The weather was lovely, and she appreciated the views of places, even those already known to her, more than ever before. A highlight was visiting Durham Cathedral, which she had always wanted to see when living up north but had never managed. She found the mixture of styles in the building so fascinating: the west door area was nothing like the west end of most cathedrals, with its twelfth-century Norman Galilee Chapel, while at the east end was the thirteenth-century Gothic Chapel of the Nine Altars; and there was no grand entrance, just a door on the north side. They saw Hadrian's Wall and also the Lake District, where Joan had often been to visit an aunt.

They reached the Scottish coast at Oban via Lockerbie, took a ferry to the Island of Mull and crossed to the other side to board another ferry to the Island of Iona. The last time she had been on these waters was on the yachting holiday when she had saved a woman from choking to death. That time she had only visited Iona for the day and she had always wanted to come back. Accommodation was in 'The Bishop's House' which, although rather expensive, was not very comfortable: Joan remembers being on a bunk bed and not being able to sit up without banging her head on the ceiling, and the food was pretty basic. Iona itself, with its old abbey and ecumenical Christian community, was intriguing and beautiful. From there the pilgrims went east across Scotland again and then to the north east coast to The Holy Island of Lindisfarne. This was Joan's first visit to this tidal island on the Northumberland coast, with its castle and ruined priory. She suddenly became '*au fait* with Aidan and Cuthbert and co.'.

Pilgrimage number five, in the autumn of 2006 and again led by Bishop Michael, was in Greece and the Greek islands:

'The Steps of St Paul and St John'. It was an autumn of terrific storms, one after the other. First they flew to Athens and from there north to Thessaloniki, which Joan already knew from a swimming training trip. That second flight was very bumpy because a storm was raging. In Thessaloniki, terrible floods were washing away bridges and causing frightful devastation. The pilgrims' coach had to do huge detours. Once when they were sitting in a restaurant having lunch, water came rushing through. It was almost unbelievable. One evening a rather dejected Bishop Michael came to Joan with his clothes and leather boots, which were all wringing wet. Joan asked him what he expected her to do with them, whereupon he said that he needed to wear them the next day. Joan said that all she could do was deal with the boots, which she promptly stuffed with newspaper. He asked her where she had learnt this technique, whereupon Joan replied, as she so often did: 'The Guides'.

They travelled further south to Meteora, again already known to Joan, and famous for its extraordinary vertical rock towers topped with monasteries. Then they went on to Delphi, Corinth and Athens, and finally they were on a boat exploring the Greek islands. One Sunday they were on their way to the island of Patmos, but there was such a storm that they had to seek shelter in the harbour of a small place called Levos. Ailsie and Joan decided to go for a walk from the harbour. When they got back to the boat the Bishop said to Joan they had all been looking for her because they thought she would like to meet some local Scouts, boys and girls, who had their meetings on Sunday afternoons in the local hall. The girls, some of them quite small, were thrilled to have visitors from a boat dropping in unexpectedly. Some of the people there could manage a bit of English, but one of the pilgrims, the Greek husband of an English woman, was able to speak Greek to them. With his help the Bishop, not looking at all bishop-like in his shocking red shorts, name-dropped: Dr Martin knew the Chief Guide, so she would be most interested to see what they were doing. It worked: they were allowed to be involved with their activities all afternoon. Joan was quite impressed with what they were doing and, back in England, reported to the Guide Association who were very interested.

The Bishop was insistent that they should get to Patmos, despite the weather. It turned out to be very worthwhile. After being exiled to Patmos by the Roman Emperor Domitian in 95 AD, St John the Divine is thought to have used a cave there when he wrote the Book of Revelation. This is what people come for. It is now encased by a sanctuary and encircled by a convent, so few people are allowed access. The pilgrims had to hold their service outside. The island held other attractions: old castles and huge walls showed what a hotbed of unrest the area had been.

From there they sailed on to Symi. On their way another frightful storm of thunder, lightning and violent wind blew up. They normally ate on deck but this time the three crew asked the pilgrims to have their meal sitting inside the middle of the boat, where the crew themselves would normally have been. Suddenly the engines stopped, and while the panicking crew tried to restart them Joan and the Bishop realised that they could capsize very easily as they were now truly at the mercy of the banging, buffeting waves. Sitting around the table, Joan was on a collapsible chair, so she regularly ended up under the table. Eventually she said: 'Next time this happens I'm staying under the table as this is getting silly.' All the pilgrims looked terrified; they were not wearing life jackets and had not even been told where they were, if indeed they existed at all. Joan did not think there was much chance of surviving if they ended up in the sea, but she was already planning who she would try to save if it happened. She knew that the Bishop's wife, Cynthia, could not swim and was terrified of water, so she decided she would try to save her. After what seemed an age the engines were restarted and the boat continued without mishap. When Joan told the Bishop about her intention to save his wife he responded jokingly: 'What, not me?' The Bishop felt that it would be appropriate to sing a hymn after having been saved. Joan was determined that it should not be 'Eternal Father, strong to save', and quickly suggested 'Praise God from whom all blessings flow' which they duly sang as best they could without hymn books.

Although they had booked a mooring in the harbour at Symi, so many boats had come to shelter from the storm that there was no room, so they had to anchor out in the middle of the bay. The storm raged all night. At the beginning of the trip some of the pilgrims were sea-sick, but by this time they had got their sea legs, or perhaps they were too frightened to be sick, thought Joan. She was very thankful that she was a good sailor. The next morning they saw with dismay that huge amounts of precious soil had been washed down from the interior of the rocky island, soil that the people could not afford to lose. The pilgrims were scheduled to cross to the other side of the island by coach to a monastery. At first they were told that this was impossible because of landslides, but again the Bishop was insistent. The journey was much delayed by numerous boulders that had to be moved out of the way at various stages along the road. Perhaps Bishop Michael was so insistent because the monastery was St Michael's.

2009 saw Joan's return visit to Iona, lasting just under a week. This, her sixth pilgrimage, was led by the Revd Rob Marshall, and Joan and two others were parishioners of St Mary Abbots Church. This visit was a retreat, and for Joan it was an incredible experience. The party travelled by rail to York and then by coach across the north of England and part of Scotland, including Loch Lomond, to Oban, Mull and Iona. This time, instead of the 'holy poverty' of The Bishop's House, they were housed in beautifully converted cottages offering bed and breakfast, while excellent meals were on offer in a pub each evening. The pilgrims were blessed with good weather. One day Joan went on an extra boat trip to the island of Staffa on a beautiful calm, sunny day, where they were allowed to scramble up onto the rocks. She asked the skipper if the summer there had been bad, as in England; he said no, adding that English people tended to think Scotland suffered bad weather, but when England was awash with rain they were often basking under blue skies. Joan had always been lucky when visiting Scotland, starting with her first trip by yacht from Liverpool.

On a Friday, the day before the party was due to leave Iona, a serious storm was forecast. Schoolchildren from Mull were recalled before the end of the week so that they would not be stranded. The pilgrims were told that if they did not leave by the seven o'clock ferry on the Saturday morning they would not get across. Joan remembers them dragging their cases to the ferry in the dark. They were able to cross and returned by coach to York, this time travelling across Scotland to Stirling on the way. Iona had been magical for Joan, and another wonderful chance to study the Celtic saints. The pilgrimage, with its better accommodation, was such a success that the Revd Rob Marshall repeated it in 2010. Unfortunately the weather then was so dreadful that journeys were disrupted and delayed; Joan was glad that she had been in 2009.

In May 2010 Joan went on her seventh pilgrimage, to the passion play at Oberammergau, a small town in Bavaria. She had been aware of the play all her life because her father had taken parties to it, but although she had always wanted to go, the time had never been right. The background to the play is that in the 17th century when bubonic plague was spreading in the region, the townspeople made a bargain with God that every ten years they would perform a play about the life and death of Jesus if he spared them. The numbers of plague victims decreased rapidly and the play was first performed in 1634. Today coach loads of tourists – a few hundred thousand – pour in from all parts of the world so, in order to make sure they all see the play, it is put on five times a week from May to October, but only every ten years. The performance takes all afternoon, from 2.30 to 5 and, after a break for supper, continues in the evening from 8 until 11. Anything up to 2,000 townspeople are involved including singers, musicians and technicians, and Joan sensed there was no competition amongst them: they were a real team. Most people made their own costumes; only those worn by the principal actors were made in Munich. Shopkeepers taking part had to close their businesses for the afternoon or find someone to stand in for them, while other workers involved could only go to work in the mornings. The whole place was geared to the play. As well as the actors, a choir of about fifty all dressed in white would process in, telling the story in song, and then exit; the orchestra was out of sight. Accommodation is only available for two nights per person. Joan and four other St Mary Abbots pilgrims, including Father Rob, stayed in a chalet run by a woman who was in the play, along with her husband and two children. The performance is in the open air, although the 4,500-strong audience is under cover. Joan says the audience seemed to be in a kind of covered funnel with the open stage at the end, and behind it the mountains: a wonderful setting.

The weather was not very good and the theatre was quite cold, but Joan sat between Father Rob and her friend Pamela

Wood and they managed to hire a blanket to share. The play was in German, of course, but the audience had bilingual copies of the text. Joan wrote in an article for the parish in the Kensington Parish News: 'The crowd scenes were most exciting and included several hundred people, goats and sheep. [The play] starts with Palm Sunday and Jesus is mobbed as he rides in on a donkey. The officials – the High Priest, Pilate and the soldiers were more than difficult. I was amazed at Jesus's patience and particularly his wonderful relationship with the children, the women and the disabled. In the second half the scenes were almost too agonising to watch – the Last Supper and Jesus's friends deserting him, Peter's misery and the betrayal by Judas who finally hangs himself at the back of the stage. The flogging, the crown of thorns and ultimately the crucifixion. The play ends with the two Marys searching for the body of Jesus. The Angel says: "Who are you looking for? He has gone from here – go and tell his disciples. He will ascend to the Father. Hallelujah! He is risen!" There were no curtain calls and we walked home in the dark – through the rain.'

Joan noticed that, although it was May, the shops were selling Christmas and other religious decorations because of the play. An advantage of having lived in Adelboden was knowing how mountain villages tended to be laid out, and also what the signs over the shops signified. Looking down a side street on one occasion, she caught sight of the sign of a wood carver and went to visit the shop with Pamela, who was surprised that she had known what it was. They bought lots of small items as gifts to take home; the carver's wife served them and was delighted that they had found the shop, which not many tourists managed. The woman's family were all either actors in the play or in the orchestra. The pilgrims went to the shop the next day and the carver's wife was so impressed at their enthusiasm that she called her husband out of his workshop to meet them.

After their two nights in Oberammergau, the party moved on to Strobl in the Austrian Alps for five days, from where they went on a day trip to Salzburg and also an evening visit for a Mozart concert. The weather had not improved so the mountains were scarcely visible, but the lakes and lakeside towns were lovely. In Strobl itself they had a free morning to do what they wanted. Some of the party decided to go up a mountain by funicular railway but Joan stayed behind, knowing from her time in Adelboden that it was pointless going up a mountain in cloud. She was amused by the exclamations of surprise on their return at not having been able to see anything. That same morning Joan and Pamela by chance met a couple who suggested a leisurely tourist ride together in one of the horse-drawn carriages. From the carriage they had a wonderful view not only of the small town with its riverside churches but also of fields of wonderful wild flowers, knee-high – kingcups, daisies, bugle, campions and dandelions. During the ride it emerged that the couple were friends of Bishop Michael. Quite a coincidence.

9. Up to Date

Before she moved to her present flat just off Earls Court Road, Joan lived for many years in a lovely little one up two flights of stairs above a shop in Kensington Church Street. She liked the location, close to the places she wanted to get to, but the stairs were becoming harder for her to cope with because of her painful knees. On the first floor was a studio which a lady artist used during the day only, but for quite some time Joan also had a male neighbour living above her. She was on good terms with him, and she liked knowing that there was a man in the house. He was a pleasant, dapper gentleman but he obviously had a drink problem. One Sunday morning, the morning after the 'Last Night at the Proms' which Joan had watched on television, Joan went down the stairs to go to church and, near the bottom, saw two feet sticking up the stairs with a body behind them, its head up against the front door. It was her gentleman neighbour. He was clearly dead and had probably fallen down the stairs backwards, cracking his skull or breaking his neck against the door. She had not heard him fall perhaps because she had been watching the Proms. Her first thought was an extraordinary one: that she would be accused of having killed him, as she was the only other person in the house. Joan thinks that she had this thought because, although not legally trained, she has a tendency to think as a lawyer would. She pulled herself together and went down to make absolutely sure he was dead before going back up to her flat to ring the police.

When they arrived, after Joan assured them that her neighbour was past help, they then spent a long time trying to force their way into the building. The space was tight and it was impossible to open the front door without moving the body, which Joan could not manage to do. Eventually

111

the police were able to open the door just enough for a slim policewoman to squeeze in – to the unpleasant scrunching sound of more bones breaking. Joan had been planning to take lunch to a great Guide friend, Patricia Ostler, in Hampstead after church; Patricia was disabled and also diabetic, so she needed her food on time. When Joan rang to explain what was happening, Pat said: 'You are the giddy limit, what will you get up to next!' Joan finally got to Patricia by about two o'clock, after giving the police a statement. She was amazed that they never questioned her again and that she did not have to attend an inquest; in fact she thought it a bit too trusting of them: as a doctor she had had experience of children whose deaths had had to be investigated. Unpleasant but necessary.

Except when the artist was downstairs, Joan was then mostly alone in the house for some time, while the top flat was being done up. Although she never felt lonely there, her friends were getting worried that the stairs were proving too much. Bishop Michael and his wife Cynthia were so concerned that they spoke to her about it, 'nagging' her about the stairs and pretending that they could hardly manage them themselves. Joan, of course, did not want to leave Kensington and got many brochures about sheltered or semi-sheltered accommodation in the borough. When she had selected about a dozen places she might consider, Cynthia kindly typed all the letters of application for her. Unfortunately it turned out that Joan was not eligible for any of them because, owning a flat, she was a lady of too much substance. She started searching for a flat through estate agents and was getting nowhere when the Bishop asked the Revd Rob Marshall to put his mind to the problem.

Father Rob really took the task seriously and found Joan's present flat on the internet. Although not 'sheltered', it is in a block that has lifts and porters – 'they are my friends in this building'. Father Rob, the Bishop and Cynthia used all their powers of persuasion, insisting that Joan move there, and in the end she surrendered, but not before she had asked Patrick Hastings to visit the flat and check that he could reach it in his wheelchair. She also asked John Scott to approve it; he had phoned her regularly as he was also quite worried about her accommodation. With the help of her solicitor and advice from Father Rob, she sold her old flat, which the owners of the shop on the ground floor were keen to acquire. Her new flat was furnished, which she had not really wanted, so she had to give away most of her own furniture that she had had since her student days. The process took two years.

Joan is gradually getting to know one or two neighbours. She goes to a nearby weekly exercise class and has met some local residents there. One is Dorothy Baldwin, who lives in the next block of flats. Great was Joan's surprise when she attended a lecture and supper at Apothecaries' Hall in April 2011 and met Dorothy there: it turned out that Dorothy, being a medical author, was also an Apothecary. Joan's life is full of coincidences. Another local resident at their exercise class was Diana Midgley, parishioner of the local St Philip's Church. Tragically Diana was killed while crossing Cromwell Road. Joan and Dorothy met at her funeral on 4 April only to meet again two days later at Apothecaries' Hall.

2010 was a dreadful year for Joan in terms of losing friends and relatives: she seemed constantly to be going to funerals. She worries about her foster sister, Barbara, who is bravely fighting cancer, and her sister Beryl, who is suffering from Alzheimer's disease. As already mentioned, Beryl and Joan did not have much in common and therefore tended not to see each other very often. Beryl always seemed to be more of a mother's girl, although she had a teaching career and even advised Phyllis Gordon Spencer, head of the girls' programme of the Duke of

Edinburgh's Award Scheme, on the home economics section of the award. For years Beryl's husband, Philip Hammond, had appeared to resent Joan's success in her life and work, and had never seemed to go out of his way to make her feel welcome when she visited. Then, early in February 2011, she heard that he had had a series of mini-strokes. He and Beryl were now living together in a care home. Joan went to visit them and met quite a different brother-in-law. He was utterly miserable at being in the home and said he was afraid of seeing his wife in case she did not recognise him. He had lost all his previous defiance and desperately sought comfort from Joan, for the whole two hours holding her hand, and even asking her how her Guiding and swimming were going. Joan, however, did see her sister who recognised her. Six days later Beryl's husband was dead, and Joan had another funeral to go to. Dallas, his daughter by his first wife, drove Joan to Bournemouth for the cremation service which, to her relief, was taken by a priest who gave the address, and there were two hymns. A buffet lunch in a pub followed. Beryl was not at the funeral but Joan visited her afterwards. Perhaps mercifully, she was not aware of what had happened.

On 24 May 2007, at the end of a confirmation service at St Mary Abbots Church, Joan was presented with the St Mellitus Medal by her great friend Bishop Michael. It came as a huge surprise to her, for she had not been told this was to happen. The Order of St Mellitus is conferred upon a person who has made a substantial contribution to the Christian life of London. It is named after the Bishop of London who refounded the London Diocese in AD 604 after the city had reverted to paganism following the Saxon invasions.

John Scott says that he gets a warm feeling in Joan's presence, that she is 'eternally and immaculately unselfish, commanding unheralded respect and love', that she is 'without a trumpet a glorious Christian in her all, proclaiming Christ in the quietest way'. Father Andrew Bishop, a former curate of St Mary Abbots Church, says that Joan is 'a force to be reckoned with, in the nicest possible way' and goes on to say: 'I give thanks for Joan's no-nonsense approach to life and her practical sense.'

As has been described in Chapter 1, the flame has been a very important symbol in Joan's life since she took part in the flame ceremonies at her Methodist boarding school, Hunmanby Hall. At Hunmanby there was also much emphasis on the importance of the Holy Ghost, and Joan saw, and still sees, the flame as a symbol of this Spirit. Although the granddaughter of a fire-fighter, she is afraid of fire when it is out of control, but finds it full of spiritual significance when it is not. At difficult times it has often been a great comfort and reassurance to her.

As a young woman Joan was once running a Guide camp on English heathland scattered with birch trees. It was afternoon and Joan was conducting a 'Guides' Own', the informal, ecumenical service held at camps without clergy. These services were about 45 minutes long and consisted of readings, prayers, reflections and sometimes music; they often had a theme, and on this occasion the theme was the Holy Ghost. The Guides were sitting in their customary horseshoe around the camp fire, which had been stamped out the evening before. Joan was just reflecting out loud on the theme of the Holy Ghost, often symbolised by fire, when something extraordinary happened: the camp fire suddenly flared up as spent fires sometimes will, but these new flames were so violent that there was a risk that the surrounding heath and birches would catch light. Immediately buckets of water had to be brought and poured on to the flames, which fortunately subsided. The service was abandoned, but Joan felt that this was probably the nearest thing to a miracle she had ever experienced.

Was God perhaps telling Joan that she was in tune with him? She has dedicated her whole life to helping people, passing the flame and being faithful to her religious beliefs. In the spirit of the last line of Joan's school hymn it can be said of her: 'Lord, she is true to thee!'